English
for the
World of Work

by

Carolyn W. Knox

American Guidance Service
Circle Pines, Minnesota 55014-1796

About the Author

Carolyn W. Knox received her undergraduate degree from Towson State University and her master's degree from Loyola College. She has also done considerable course work at American, Temple, and Johns Hopkins University. Before she retired in July of 1990, Mrs. Knox had served twenty-seven years in the Baltimore City Public Schools as a secondary English teacher, demonstration teacher, and English department head. For the last fifteen years of her career, she was supervisor of English and elementary language arts, head of English textbook adoption, and director of English and language arts curriculum production. In addition to learning packages, workbooks, and textbooks, Mrs. Knox has written critiques and other materials as a consultant for several leading educational publishing houses.

Staff

Norm Myers, Design
Carol Munschauer, Artwork

Printed in the United States of America

ISBN: 0-88671-532-6 (Previously ISBN: 0-7916-0082-3)

Order Number: 80160

A 0 9 8 7 6

Contents

CHAPTER 1

Finding Your Career

Jim Addison needs a full-time job. The jobs Jim had before were part-time jobs that he got by reading signs in store windows. He had learned to type before he graduated from school. Now he wants a permanent job. His friends tell him to read the *classified ads* in the newspapers and to go to job placement centers. When Jim looks at the *help-wanted ads* in the newspaper, he wishes that he could understand them better.

Lesson 1: Reading the Help-Wanted Ads

Help-wanted ads can be hard to read. If people were more familiar with the terms and abbreviations used, ads would be much easier to understand.

Look at the example of a help-wanted ad shown on the top of the next page. Jim saw this ad in the paper. Notice the terms used to describe this particular job opening.

1

CLERK-TYPIST Fast-growing pipe, valve & fitting distributor loc on W side. Exc typ skills & exp in gen off duties a must. Call Ms. Hollins, Mon or Tues 8-10 a.m., 555-6857.

Jim understands that the ad is for a clerk-typist. He thinks that he can do this kind of work. The company that needs a clerk-typist is a distributor of pipes, valves, and fittings. Jim does not know much about that type of work, but he is sure he will learn more about it if he gets the job. The words "loc on W side" are puzzling. Jim goes to his friend, Tony, to talk about the help-wanted ad.

"Tony, would you read this ad for a clerk-typist? It may be a job I can do, but I'm not sure," Jim asked.

"Sure, Jim," answered Tony. "It says that a business located on the west side of town wants to hire a clerk-typist. You must have excellent typing skills and experience in general office duties."

"Do you think that they would count part-time experience?" asked Jim.

"I don't know, but why don't you call Ms. Hollins and ask her? You can call Monday or Tuesday between 8 o'clock and 10 o'clock in the morning."

Tony made sense out of that ad. He understood the terms and abbreviations used. You need to be able to do the same thing if you are looking for a job.

Activity A: Read these three ads. Try to figure out what the underlined words mean from the way that they are used in each ad.

1. | COOK exp'd. Cook w/refs. needed for busy restaurant nr. college. Practical exp. making soups and din. items. 235-4542.

2. | MAINTENANCE ASS'T.   Must have at least 3 yrs. exp. in htg. and AC.   All phases of maintenance nec. 542-4891.

3. | SALES   Nat'l Co, high comm.   New product. No exp. nec. Mon. 555-8695.

Activity B: Underlined words from the ads in Activity A are listed below. Match the meanings with these words. Number your paper from 1 to 13. Next to each number, write the letter of the correct meaning.

Words	**Meanings**
1. exp'd.	a. high commission
2. w/refs.	b. with references
3. nr. college	c. no experience necessary
4. exp.	d. call 555-8695 on Monday
5. din. items	e. assistant
6. ASS'T.	f. experienced
7. 3 yrs. exp.	g. three years experience
8. htg. and AC	h. national company
9. nec.	i. heating and air conditioning
10. Nat'l Co	j. near college
11. high comm.	k. dinner items
12. No exp. nec.	l. necessary
13. Mon. 555-8695	m. experience

More Abbreviations in Help-Wanted Ads

There are other terms and abbreviations that you and Jim will need to know before you can fully understand help-wanted ads. *Abbreviations* are shortened forms for written words. Study this list carefully.

aft.	— afternoon	ins.	— insurance
agcy.	— agency	lic.	— license
avail.	— available	mfg.	— manufacturing
beg.	— beginning	min.	— minimum
bene.	— benefits	pd.	— paid
des.	— desired	pos.	— position
ed.	— education	pref.	— preferred
eve.	— evenings	p/t	— part time
exc.	— excellent	req.	— required
f/t	— full time	sal.	— salary
grad.	— graduate	trng.	— training
incl.	— including/included	20K	— $20,000

Activity C: Rewrite these ads on your paper. Do not use abbreviations. Write every word in full. Use the list given above to help you.

1. | DRIVER Lic. req. Must work aft. & eve. Sal. and tips. Ins. and other bene. provided. 757-0853. |

2. | SECRETARY Pos. avail for high school grad with exp. Sal. 20K incl. pd. vacation and ed. bene. Must wk. f/t and some eve. 569-7588. |

3. | P/T CLERK Mfg. co. Will provide trng. Beg. min. wage. Exp. pref. Hrs. 2-6 aft. 477-3745. |

Lesson 2: How Help-Wanted Ads Are Arranged

Once you understand the terms and abbreviations used in the help-wanted ads, you need to know how these ads are organized in most newspapers. The help-wanted ads are located in the classified section. The section containing advertisements for jobs is usually called "Help Wanted" or "Employment." Within the "Help Wanted" portion, jobs are listed in alphabetical order. "Artist" would come before "clerk." "Janitor" would come before "waitress."

CLASSIFIED ADVERTISING	
Employment	
Help Wanted **(905)**	**Help Wanted** **(905)**
ADMINISTRATIVE SECY — This top Co. needs polished sect'l talents! Good skills and figure aptitude. 837-0778.	CHEF-PASTRY 4 yrs. exp. required, knowledge of European pastry pref. Send resumé to BOX CS 47822.
AIR COND & Heat Pump Mechanic fully exp. only. Call Frosty Refrig. Mondays, 747-2024.	CLERICAL If you love to type, my firm needs your skills. Excellent Salary & Benefits. Call Lisa 539-5804.
AUTO SALESPERSON Sell and make big money on cars and trucks. Salary plus comm. Benefits. 466-1320.	CLERK-TYPIST General office work, 5 days, vic. Smallwood St. 566-5806.
BOOKKEEPER With aptitude to operate bkkpg machine. Dependable. 675-1118.	COMPUTER OPERATOR To work part time eves. Must love to type. WP exp. pref. Pleasant atmosphere, free parking. Call 9-5 at 358-TYPE.

Look at the classified section of your newspaper. Find the Help Wanted part. Notice how ads are listed. You will see ads for dental assistants, mechanics, nurses, secretaries, typists, and many other kinds of jobs. These ads are listed in an order that follows the alphabet.

When Jim Addison first looked at the want ads, he was curious about how they were listed. He asked his friend, Tony, about them. Tony explained that the ads are listed in alphabetical order.

What Is Alphabetical Order?

"What do you mean by *alphabetical order?*" asked Jim.

"Well, the jobs are listed in the same order as the alphabet. That means that jobs that start with 'A' would be listed first. Jobs that start with 'B' would be second, and so on," Tony explained.

"That seems to make sense, but I wish I could practice," said Jim.

"Sure," said Tony. "Try this."

A B C D E F G H I J K L M N O P Q R S T U V W X Y Z

Activity A: Rewrite the words listed below in alphabetical order.

typist	journeyman	manager	librarian	dentist	clerk
mechanic	programmer	rater	waitress	auditor	icer
evaluator	salesperson	bartender	helper	guard	cook

"What do you do if several jobs start with the same letter?" Jim wanted to know.

"Then you look at the second letter. If 'bookkeeper' and 'bartender' are two jobs in the ads, 'bartender' would be listed first because the second letter is 'a.' 'Bookkeeper' would come after 'bartender' because the second letter is 'o,' and that letter comes later in the alphabet.

"If the first two letters are the same, you have to look at the third letter, and so on. If several job titles have more than one word and the first words are the same, you have to look at the second words. If one ad is for 'auto mechanic' and the other for an 'auto attendant,' 'auto attendant' would come first because the second word begins with 'a.' "

Now, you try to do something that's harder. Remember what Tony told Jim about alphabetical order. When words start with the same letter, you have to look at the second letter.

Activity B: Rewrite the words given below in alphabetical order.

mechanic	doctor	salesperson	machinist
secretary	bookkeeper	milliner	dentist
biller	banker	stenographer	buyer

Are you ready for the hardest kind of alphabetical order? Remember that if the second letters are the same, you look at the third letter, and so on. When first words are the same, you look at the second word.

Activity C: Rewrite these words and phrases in alphabetical order.

Sales	Drywall Superintendent
Engineer, Industrial	Auto Mechanic
Secretarial Lab Aide	Engineer, Electrical
Drywall Finisher	Secretarial Assistant
Dry Cleaner	Engineer, Mechanical
Secretary	Executive Director
Engineer, Civil	Administrative Assistant
Auto Salesperson	Auto Repairs

The Skill of Alphabetizing

The skill of alphabetizing is an important one. It will help you to locate information in the classified ads, but it also has many other uses. The names in a *telephone directory* and the businesses described in the *Yellow Pages* are listed in alphabetical order. So are the items in *indexes* in books and book catalogs in libraries. Store directories, *reference books* like dictionaries and encyclopedias, rows of seats in an auditorium, records in record stores, and street directories are all listed in alphabetical order. Being able to find things arranged in the same order as the alphabet is a skill that you will use often.

Activity D: Look at the list of job titles given below. They were taken from the "Help Wanted" section of a newspaper. Copy these job titles in the order in which they would appear in the newspaper.

ENGINEER, ELECTRICAL
SALESPERSON
NURSE
RECEPTIONIST
CLAIMS SUPERVISOR
RETAIL SALESPERSON
ELECTRICIAN
DIETITIAN
RESEARCH ASSISTANT
TYPIST
CLERK
ANIMAL HANDLER
ENGINEER, CHEMICAL
ENGINEER, MANUFACTURING

Lesson 3: Understanding Help-Wanted Ads

You have worked with the abbreviations used in help-wanted ads. You know how the ads are arranged in the newspaper. Now you need some practice in reading and understanding these ads. Think about Jim Addison's situation again. He has had some typing. Not every ad for a clerk will be a job that Jim can do or that he will want.

Activity A: Read these ads. Then answer the following questions.

#1.

> CLERK Gen. off. duties and proofrdg. Must have good grammar skills and type 50 WPM. Apply in person 9–4 p.m. 20 E. Main St.

#2.

> CLERK 10-key touch, math aptitude a must. Typ. req. Apply by mail Box 45867, Chicago 60647.

#3.

> CLERK No exp. nec. Will train. 40-hr. wk. Mon-Fri 8 to 4. Many bene. inc. health ins. Call Mr. Merton, 555-1921.

1. Which job requires that you be able to type 50 words per minute. If Jim types 40 words per minute, should he apply for this job?
2. For which job do you apply in person?
3. For which job do you apply by phone?
4. For which job do you apply by letter?
5. In which job must you be able to proofread?
6. For which job do you need to be good in math?
7. Which ad describes a benefit the employee will receive?
8. To what address would you send your letter applying for the job described in Ad #2?
9. How would you apply for the job in Ad #3?

Jim Addison has learned to understand the terms and abbreviations used in many ads. Still, some ads in the "Help Wanted" section are tricky. Tony told him to try writing out the ads in his own words. That practice helped Jim to understand even more about help-wanted ads.

Activity B: Read each ad. Then rewrite it in your own words.

1. | SALES Outside sales in off. equip. Sal. and comm. Co. bene. Call Sally, 555-8943. |

2. | AUTO SALES Immed. pos. Exp. pref. Exc. pay plan & bene. Call for appt. 934-1012. |

Lesson 4: Do I Qualify for This Job?

In order to use the help-wanted ads wisely, you must also know whether or not you qualify for the job advertised. You will be wasting your time if you apply for jobs for which you do not have the skills. For example, Jim Addison has experience as a sales clerk and in answering the phone. He can type about 40 words per minute. He is not very good in math and has never studied shorthand. When he looks at ads, he would not bother with the ones that say the applicant must be good in math or the ones that say the person needs to be able to take shorthand.

How can you decide whether or not you can do a job? Listed on pages 10 and 11 are several ideas you need to think about.
1. Do I have the education required?
2. Can I work the hours and days listed?
3. Do I have the skills needed?

4. Am I able to work the machinery needed for this job?
5. Can I use the tools needed to do this job?
6. Do I have all the other requirements needed for this job?

Is This Job Suitable for Me?

When you apply for a job, you need to think about the personal satisfaction that working at that job could bring. You need to decide if this is the kind of job that you would like to do. Think about how you would enjoy working at this job day after day. Ask yourself the following questions:

1. Is this the kind of job that I will enjoy doing?
2. Is the salary enough to meet my needs and to make me feel good about the work I'm doing?
3. Can I get to this place easily so that I am never late?

Your career is very important. The kind of start you get can make the difference between being a success or a failure. You want to make very sure that you answer ads that describe the best job for you.

Study the help-wanted ads in your newspaper. Use the questions on pages 10 and 11 to help you decide whether or not you are qualified for the jobs described in the ads. Use the questions in this section to decide if a job is suitable for you. You probably won't be able to answer all these questions. Employers do not always list *salary*, complete *benefits* like vacation or insurance, possibilities for advancement, and other information in want ads.

You want to pick a job you can work for a period of time. Most employers do not like to hire people who change jobs too often.

Activity A: Read this help-wanted ad.   Then read about the three people described below. Decide which person is best qualified to do the job. Decide which person will probably be best at the job. Be ready to discuss the reasons for your decisions.

> ASST. CARPENTER'S HELPER No exp. nec. Must have knowledge of tools and talent for this kind of work. Perm. pos. Opp. for advancement to good worker. Must have driver's lic. Apply in person. Ace Company, 115 Orange Street.

1. Bob enjoys working with his hands. He knows how to use most tools and fixes all the small appliances in his home. He lives on a bus line that goes right by Ace Company. It will take him about 30 minutes to get there. He can work any hours. He also has a license and can drive a car.

2. Maggie went to a vocational school and majored in carpentry. She is skilled with most of the tools used by a carpenter. She has a car and can drive to Ace Company in about 35 minutes. If she has to take the bus, it will take her an hour. She can work any hours that the company wants employees to work.

3. Jud needs a job. He can use simple tools. He really likes meeting people and working with them. He has a car and a license and can get to the Ace Company in about 15 minutes. He is not sure that he will like this job, but he needs to earn more money.

Lesson 5: Employment Agencies and Job Placement Offices

Jim Addison thought about going to an *employment agency* or to a job placement office. These places are in business to help people find jobs. However, most employment agencies charge a fee payable after you have been hired. That fee can be as much as 10% of your first year's pay. The fee is usually paid by the person looking for the job. Sometimes the employer offers to pay the fee. Before you sign with an agency, make sure you find out who pays the fee and what the fee is. You may find that it is worth paying a fee to get a job. If you cannot afford a fee, stay away from an agency where the fee is paid by the employee.

The best way to find an employment agency is to look in the Yellow Pages of the telephone directory and study the ads. Many agencies specialize in only certain kinds of jobs. You want to make sure that an agency will be able to get you the job you want. Many of the ads also tell whether the employee or the employer will pay the fee.

Activity A: Look at this ad. Then answer the following questions.

JOB SEARCH, INC.
For assistance in your office and for
professional job placement

Stenographers, bookkeepers, receptionists, typists

Fee Paid by Employers

2313 Kansas Street 555-1438

---

1. Could this agency help you find a job as an automobile mechanic?
2. Jim Addison can type. Would this agency be able to help him?
3. Would Jim have to pay the agency's fee?
4. What is the name of this agency? Where is it located?
5. What telephone number should Jim call to get more information?

Job Placement Offices

Some places that can help you to look for a job do not charge a fee. Most states and many large cities have *job placement offices.* At these offices you can fill out an application and talk with a counselor. The *counselor* will give you advice and work with you to help you find a job. The United States government has an Office of Personnel Management. You can go to this office to apply for jobs with the government. You will also probably have to take a test for a government job. The telephone numbers of these kinds of job placement offices are listed in the telephone directory.

Jim Addison went to his state's employment center. He found that he could get all kinds of help at the center at no charge to him. Many state and city employment centers offer the same types of help that the one in Jim's state does.

The following list describes services offered by employment centers run by city and state governments.

- The center has a list of job openings sent to them by employers. After interviews with trained counselors, people who seem to be able to do a particular job are sent for *job interviews.* At these interviews, an employer can decide if the person being interviewed would be good to hire.

- People who want jobs in some trades can be placed in *apprenticeship programs.* In these programs people are trained while they work on the job. They gain practical experience under the supervision of skilled workers.

- People can get information about jobs available all over the country, not just in their city or state.

- If people are not sure what they can do or what they want to do, job counselors can still help them. Job counselors may even give people tests to see what they do best and to learn more about their abilities and interests.

When Jim was first interviewed by a counselor, he was uncomfortable. He thought the counselor was asking too many personal questions. After a while Jim realized that the counselor needed to ask such questions. From the answers the counselor could more easily match Jim with the best job.

Many employment centers may ask you to fill out a *job application*. This form is used in making a request to be hired. The information you have to supply is like the information you give on any job application. Following the steps in Chapter 4 of this book will help you do a good job on the application you fill out at an employment center.

Activity B: Answer these questions.
1. Where would you go to apply for work with the U.S. government?
2. Do you have to pay a fee at employment centers run by the state or city?
3. How do the centers get their list of available jobs?
4. Where can you find the telephone numbers of these employment centers?
5. Why do counselors interview people who want jobs?
6. What is an apprenticeship program?
7. Why might you want information about jobs available in other cities and states?
8. Why would a counselor give you a test?

Summary

You need certain skills just to find a job that you can do. Two skills you need to know are how to read ads from the "Help Wanted" section of the newspaper and how to understand what the ads mean. Then you must know if you can do the job they advertise.

Help-wanted ads are placed in alphabetical order, usually by the name of the job. These ads use many abbreviations to get a lot of information in a small space. Knowing the abbreviations that are used most often will help you to read and to understand the ads.

Then you must decide if you can do the job. Do you have the skills that the job requires, such as working with certain machinery or using certain tools? You will also want to think about whether this is a job you'll like doing and whether the job will pay enough money to meet your needs.

In addition to using ads, you can also get a job through employment agencies and job placement offices. Employment agencies charge a fee for finding you a job. Job placement offices are government offices and do not charge a fee.

In this chapter both you and Jim Addison learned more about the "Help Wanted" section of the classified ads. You discovered the meanings of many abbreviations that are used in these ads. You saw that the help-wanted ads are arranged in alphabetical order. You practiced reading and using information from these ads. The review activities for this chapter will provide more practice in the skills you learned.

CHAPTER REVIEW

Review Activity A: Review your understanding of ad abbreviations.

1. Rewrite these two ads. Replace the abbreviations with complete words.

    a.
    > DRIVER Coll. stu. w/car. P/t, Tues. and Thurs. Must have good driving record. Refs. req. No exp. nec. Pos. avail. immed. Call Jones Mfg. Co., 555-4635. 2-4 p.m.

    b.
    > SALES   Exp'd. w/refs.   High comm.   Must be h.s. grad. F/t, eves. Good sal. Bene. incl. ins. Apply in pers. 8900 Business Blvd.

2. Select an ad from the help-wanted section of your newspaper. Rewrite it without using abbreviations.

Review Activity B: Rewrite these job titles in alphabetical order.

Pediatric Instructor   Construction Supervisor
Sales Representative   Pediatric Assistant
Optical Engineer   Sales Secretary
Program Analyst   Program Manager
Cosmetic Demonstrator   Cosmetic Sales
Pediatric Nurse   Sales Trainee
Optician   Construction Superintendent
Purchasing Agent   Purchasing Chief
Occupational Therapist   Production Chief
Optometrist   Construction Manager

Review Activity C: Read the following ad carefully. Then list four qualifications that a person would need to apply for this job.

ADMINISTRATIVE CLERK-TYPIST Should have exc. typ. skills & at least some exp. w/word processing equipment. Grammar & math skills are req. Exc. sal., bene. Call Sue at 555-0653 bet. 10 a.m. & noon, Mon & Tues.

Review Activity D: Answer the following questions.

1. Where can you find information about jobs that are available? List at least three ways to find a job.
2. What services are provided at employment centers run by cities or states? List at least four.
3. What questions should you ask yourself to see if you should apply for a particular job? List at least five.
4. What things should you know about an employment agency before you ask them to help you find a job?
5. In what part of the paper can you find ads for jobs?
6. In what order are these ads arranged?
7. What three things should you think about in order to decide if a job suits your needs?
8. Why do you think employers do not like to hire people who change jobs often?
9. How can the Yellow Pages of the telephone directory help you to find a job?
10. If you were looking in the telephone book for these three agencies, which would be listed first? Which would be listed second? Which would be listed last?
    Barker Job Agency   Baker Job Agency   Berke Job Associates, Inc.

CHAPTER 2

Applying by Letter

When Wendy Ashbrook applied by letter for three jobs and didn't get any of them, she was concerned. She went to her teacher at night school and asked him what she should do. The teacher, Mr. Collins, looked at the carbon copies of the three letters Wendy had written. He knew right away why she had not gotten the jobs.

"Wendy, you need to learn something about writing *letters of application* when you want to be hired for a job. I believe you didn't get the jobs because your letters didn't follow the correct form and didn't say the right things."

"What can I do to learn how to write a letter that will get me a job?" Wendy asked.

"Come to class a half an hour early for the next few weeks, and I will give you some extra help," promised Mr. Collins.

Wendy really cared about getting a good job. She was determined. Every evening for three weeks, she went to class early to get help from Mr. Collins. During the first few evenings, Wendy learned about the parts of a business letter.

Lesson 1: The Parts of a Business Letter

Business letters may differ in form, but they all have seven basic parts:

1. Return Address
2. Date
3. Inside Address
4. Salutation, or Greeting
5. Body
6. Complimentary Close
7. Signature

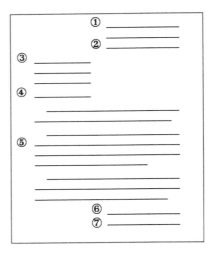

1. The *return address* begins with your house number and street name. On the next line directly underneath comes the city and state in which you live, plus your *ZIP code*. This number is used to identify postal delivery areas in the United States.

2. The *date* on which you write the letter should be written directly under your address. The return address and date should look like this example: 1230 Girard Drive
   Houston, Texas 77044
   November 24, 1999

3. The *inside address* includes the complete name and address of the person and/or the company to which the letter is being written.

    Example: Ms. Julia Evans
                         Division of Personnel
                         Landers Advertising Agency
                         1600 West South Street
                         Louisville, Kentucky 40201

4. The *salutation* is a way of greeting the person to whom you are writing. In a business letter, the salutation should be formal. It is followed by a colon.

    Example: Dear Ms. Evans:

5. The *body* of the letter tells why you are writing. Read the following example of a letter written in answer to a help-wanted ad.

       I would like to reply to your advertisement for a cashier that appeared in <u>The Evening Chronicle</u>. I am a recent graduate of Samuel Jones High School. While I was in school, I helped to run the school store. I have over two years of experience in using a cash register.

       In addition, I am good in math and careful with business machines. I like meeting people and am polite and considerate.

       I would very much like to come in for an interview. Please call me at 555-3211.

6. The *complimentary close* is a way of ending the letter politely. In a business letter, the complimentary close should be formal. It is followed by a comma.

    Example: Yours very truly,

7. The *signature* tells the person receiving the letter who you are. Your signature should be neat and easy to read. On a business letter, it is common to include a handwritten signature above a typed full name.

Example: *Wendy Ashbrook*
Wendy Ashbrook

After Wendy had studied the parts of the business letter, Mr. Collins gave her a test. See how well you understand the seven parts of a business letter.

Activity A: Number your paper from 1 to 7. Match the parts of a letter in the first column with the correct description in the second column. Write the correct letter next to each number. See if you can do this activity without looking back in the book to find the answers.

Parts of a Letter
1. return address
2. signature
3. salutation
4. date
5. complimentary close
6. inside address
7. body

Description
a. tells the person who you are
b. a way of greeting the person to whom you are writing
c. has your address and the city and state where you live
d. tells why you are writing
e. includes the name and address of the person to whom you are writing
f. tells when the letter was written
g. is a polite way of closing your letter

Activity A: Read the following letter. Then number your paper from 1 to 7. Write the correct name of the letter part next to each number.

5617 Kelly Street
Madison, Wisconsin 53701   ①
April 5, 1997 ②

Personnel Director
Clean Soap Company   ③
2 East 33rd Street
Madison, Wisconsin 53702

Dear Personnel Director: ④

I am writing to apply for the job of packer you advertised through the Wisconsin Employment Placement Center.

I have had no experience as a packer, but I learn quickly. I had a good record of attendance at Green   ⑤
Waters High where I just graduated. I was never late in four years of high school.

If you would be interested in interviewing me, I can be reached at 555-0008.

Very truly yours,   ⑥

Fred Soames

Fred Soames   ⑦

Activity B: Write your own full block style letter in answer to this ad.

MAILROOM CLERK Good rdg. skills. F/T Mon. thru. Fri., 6 a.m. to 2:30 p.m. Apply by mail, Griner, Inc., 44 Court Square, (your city).

Lesson 3: The Modified Block Style of the Business Letter

After Wendy had learned the full block style, Mr. Collins said, "Now, Wendy, there's another form you should learn. It's a bit harder, but it's the one that is used most often. It's called the *modified block style.*"

Wendy said, "Okay, Mr. Collins, tell me about this style. I'm ready. I really want to get a job."

Mr. Collins gave Wendy this skeleton of the modified block style of the business letter for her to study.

	Return Address and Date
Inside Address	
Salutation	
Body	
	Complimentary Close
	Signature

Wendy remembered that she had a letter in her purse. She showed it to Mr. Collins. "I think this is written in modified block style," said Wendy. Mr. Collins studied the letter and said, "Yes, you're right, Wendy." This is what Wendy's letter looked like.

---

47 Winslow Drive
Cedar Rapids, Iowa 52401
December 12, 1998

Ms. Wendy Ashbrook
1230 Girard Drive
Houston, Texas 77013

Dear Ms. Ashbrook:

Thank you for ordering our special digital watch. This item has been so popular that it will be three weeks before we can send the watch you ordered.

We hope this delay will not cause you any inconvenience. We know you will be glad you waited!

Very truly yours,

Harry Johnson

Harry Johnson,
Mail Order Division

Wendy noticed that several parts of the modified block style were *indented* and did not go against the margin. She also noticed that the return address, date, complimentary close, and signature were placed directly under one another. She saw that this letter was also carefully spaced.

Activity A: Shown below are parts of one letter in the modified block style. They are not placed in order, and they certainly do not look the way they should in a letter. On a sheet of paper, arrange these parts in the correct places for a modified block style letter.

4893 Layton Street
Detroit, Michigan 48233
February 1, 1999

Very truly yours,

I am interested in applying for a clerk-typist position with your company. I have had experience in this area and will be in Denver on February 10. May I come for an interview and talk with you about possible employment?

I will arrive in Denver on February 8 and will be staying at the Mile High Hotel. Please call me there.

Dear Mr. Wise:

Mr. Charles A. Wise
18 Court House Building
Denver, Colorado 80202

John Ayers
John Ayers

Activity B: Now write your own letter in modified block style. Answer the ad given below.

SCHOOL CROSSING GUARD No exp. nec. Will train. Must be able to wk Mon.-Fri. from 7:45 a.m. to 9:15 a.m. and from 2:30 p.m. to 3:30 p.m. Apply by letter to: Department of Transportation, 115 Main Street, (your city).

Lesson 4: Understanding Business Letters

You have just studied two forms of business letters: full block and modified block. The following review activities will help you understand the differences between these two forms.

Activity A: On your paper, list the seven parts of the business letter in the order in which they would be found. Arrange your answers in order from the top of the letter to the bottom.

- inside address
- body
- return address
- signature
- date
- salutation
- complimentary close

Activity B: On your paper, answer these questions about the full block form letter.

1. If you are writing a letter using full block form, where would you put your address? Where would you put your city, state, and ZIP code? Where would you put the date?

2. Where would you put the name of the person to whom you are writing?

3. Do you indent for paragraphs?

4. How many lines would you leave between each paragraph?

5. Where would you put the complimentary close?

6. Where would you put your signature?

7. Many secretaries like using the full block form because they say it is easier and that they are less likely to make mistakes. Why do you think they feel this way?

Activity C: On your paper, answer these questions about the modified block style of the business letter.

1. If you are using the modified block style, where would you put your city, state, and ZIP code? Where would you put the date?
2. Where would you put the name of the person to whom you are writing?
3. Do you indent for paragraphs?
4. How many lines would you leave between each paragraph?
5. Where would you put the complimentary close?
6. Where would you put your signature?

Activity D: Listed below are several job application situations. On your paper, list the information that you would have to include when writing a letter of application for each job.

1. You are writing to apply for the job of cabinetmaker. The employer wants a person with experience and a good record. He wants someone who has served as an apprentice in cabinetmaking and knows how to use all the tools. He wants someone he can count on to come to work regularly. You think you can handle this job. What information will you include in your letter of application?
2. You are writing to apply for the job of nurse's assistant in a hospital. The ad states that the hospital wants someone who has worked in a hospital before and who has experience in working with sick people. They also want someone who can work odd hours. You think you can handle this job. What information will you include in your letter of application?

Lesson 5: Knowing What to Say

"I've learned a lot about business letters," smiled Wendy. "You've been a big help to me."

"Well, don't relax too much," said Mr. Collins. "The hardest part is yet to come. Of course, your letter must have the correct form. However, the body of the letter is also important. It must contain the right information," he warned.

"How do I know what I should include in a letter of application?" asked Wendy.

"That's easy," said Mr. Collins. "Here is a list of five questions to ask after you have written the rough draft of your letter. If you can answer 'Yes' to all these questions, you have a good letter. Here are the questions."

1. Have I identified the job title and told exactly how I found out about the job?
2. Have I listed the skills I have that would help me do the job?
3. Have I given references if they are asked for? *References* are names of people who know you and who can describe your character, how well you do things, or how you get along with others. You might include the names of friends, teachers, clergymen, or people for whom you have worked.
4. Have I given a telephone number where I can be reached if a person from the company wants to contact me?
5. Have I told the person at the company what time I can be reached at this phone number?

Activity A: Look at the body of a letter of application given below. Then number your paper from 1 to 5. Ask the five questions shown on page 31. If you can answer "Yes" to the question, write *Yes* next to the number. If you can't, write *No*.

I read your ad for a job. I am interested in applying for this position.

I can type 50 words per minute and have good English skills. I am 28 years old. My birthday is August 30.

My references are:
Mr. John Hammond, Owner
John's Car Wash
1518 Fulton Street
Baton Rouge, Louisiana 70821

Ms. Myra Green, Teacher
Lockland High School
4000 Mars Drive
Baton Rouge, Louisiana 70824

If you would like me to come in for an interview, call me between 7 a.m. and 9 a.m. or after 5 p.m.

Knowing What to Leave Out

"It is just as important to decide what to leave out of a letter of application as it is to decide what to put in. No employer wants to read a letter full of information that has nothing to do with the job. Chances are that he will throw that kind of letter right into the wastebasket," explained Mr. Collins.

"In the body of the letter on page 32, there were two pieces of information that could have been left out—the age of the person writing and the person's birthday."

Wendy thought carefully. "How do I know what to leave out?" she asked.

"Provide the information asked for in the ad or in the job summary at the agency or placement center. If you do a complete job of that, you won't have to worry about anything else," continued Mr. Collins.

Activity B: This list of facts might be included in a letter of application. Below the list is a want ad. Decide which facts you would include in a letter answering that ad. Write *Yes* or *No* for each answer.

Clue: Remember that there are some facts you should include even if the ad doesn't ask for them.

Fact List
1. Typing skill
2. Whether or not you have a driver's license
3. Whether or not you graduated from high school
4. Your high school grades
5. Two references
6. Your good history grades
7. The award you got for perfect attendance
8. Your part-time job as a printer's helper
9. The distance between your house and the company advertising the job
10. Your telephone number

PRINTER'S ASST. h.s. grad w/exp. Have good attend. rec. Apply by letter to Good Printing Co., 487 Oak Lane, (your city).

Activity C: Here's another list of facts and another ad. Read the ad carefully.   Then decide which facts you would include in a letter answering that ad. Write *Yes* or *No* for each answer.

Fact List
1. Your good math grades
2. Your poor physical education grades
3. Your experience in helping your father keep his books
4. The time it will take you to get to work
5. That you have a new car

BOOKKEEPER Some exp. pref. Must be good in math. Driv. lic. helpful. Apply by letter. Morgan Bros., 27 Lee Ave., (your city).

Lesson 6: Writing Business Letters

"The best way to become a good letter writer is just to practice. Because the body of the letter is so important, you should practice writing bodies of letters as often as possible," advised Mr. Collins.

"Writing letters is hard work," said Wendy with a sigh.

"That's true, Wendy," said Mr. Collins, "but remember that you want to get a job. That takes hard work."

Mr. Collins is right. The letter you send to someone is a part of you. The person judges you from the way the letter looks and the way it sounds. You want to make a good impression. Therefore you will have to work hard and practice your skills. Then when someone looks at your letter, that person will think, "This is someone that I would like to hire."

Activity A: Shown below is a help-wanted ad. Write the body of the letter that you would write to apply for this job.

SALES TRAINEE for ins. co. No exp. nec. Should have good math and English skills. Answer by letter including 2 refs. to McGill Company, 904 Glenn Drive, (your city).

Lesson 7: Addressing Envelopes

Wendy practiced and practiced writing letters of application and getting the form right.

Then Mr. Collins said, "Wendy, there's one more step before you finish. You have to know the proper way to address the envelope. No matter how good your letter is, if the envelope is not addressed properly, it may not get to the person to whom you intended to send it."

Shown below is a sample envelope that Mr. Collins gave Wendy.

Ms. Ella Black
112 South Central Street
Cheyenne, Wyoming 82001

Brown, Ellis, and Company
8832 Louden Avenue
Pittsburgh, Pennsylvania 15219

Notice that the *return address* is in the upper left-hand corner of the envelope shown on page 35. The person who is sending the letter puts his or her name on the top line. On the second line is the street address. Directly under that is the city, state, and ZIP code—all on the same line.

Notice that the name and address of the company receiving the letter is several lines under the return address and considerably to the right. This arrangement gives the envelope a balanced look. The stamp, of course, would go in the upper right-hand corner.

Include the ZIP code on every letter you send. Leaving it out may delay your letter as much as three or four weeks.

Activity A: On a piece of paper, draw an envelope measuring $9^1/_2$ inches from left to right and 4 inches up and down. Use the information given below to address this envelope.

> This letter is being sent by Joseph Hall. Mr. Hall lives at 6715 Hartsfield Road in Baltimore, Maryland. His ZIP code is 21218. The letter is being sent to Henry Knight. Mr. Knight lives at 13 North Lanier Place in Trenton, New Jersey. His ZIP code is 08608.

Activity B: Select a help-wanted ad that must be answered by letter. Tape the ad to the top of a sheet of paper. Below this ad draw another envelope. Use the same measurements that you used on the envelope described in Activity A. Now pretend that you are answering the ad. Address the envelope. Use your return address and the address given in your help wanted ad.

Lesson 8: Abbreviations for State Names

Mr. Collins handed Wendy a list and said, "Sometimes you may want to abbreviate the name of a state. Here is a list of *state abbreviations*. The first abbreviation for each state is the old, regular abbreviation. Notice that each word begins with a capital letter and ends with a period."

"What is the second abbreviation?" asked Wendy.

"Each state also has a two-letter *post office abbreviation* that is used especially when computers prepare the address. This short abbreviation helps to keep the city, state, and ZIP code all on one line. The Post Office would like everyone to use the two-letter abbreviations. Notice that both letters in the post office abbreviations are capitals and that there are no periods."

"I'll keep this list handy. I'm sure I'll have to refer to it often," said Wendy.

Mr. Collins gave Wendy a word of caution. "If you are going to abbreviate, use either the old, regular form or the newer two-letter form. Do not mix the forms. Also, do not make up any abbreviations of your own."

Wendy carefully punched holes in the paper containing the list of abbreviations for state names. She put the paper into a large three-ringed looseleaf notebook where she kept all her notes about writing a letter of application. She found it was very helpful to have things in one place and in order. She could find them easily. This kind of organizing will also help Wendy when she gets a job.

Activity A: Here is the list of abbreviations that Mr. Collins gave to Wendy. Copy it carefully. File your copy so that you will have it later.

State	Abbr.	PO	State	Abbr.	PO
Alabama	Ala.	AL	Montana	Mont.	MT
Alaska	Alas.	AK	Nebraska	Neb.	NB
Arizona	Ariz.	AZ	Nevada	Nev.	NV
Arkansas	Ark.	AR	New Hampshire	N.H.	NH
California	Calif.	CA	New Jersey	N.J.	NJ
Colorado	Colo.	CO	New Mexico	N. Mex.	NM
Connecticut	Conn.	CT	New York	N.Y.	NY
Delaware	Del.	DE	North Carolina	N.C.	NC
District of Columbia	D.C.	DC	North Dakota	N. Dak.	ND
Florida	Fla.	FL	Ohio	O.	OH
Georgia	Ga.	GA	Oklahoma	Okla.	OK
Hawaii	H.I.	HI	Oregon	Oreg.	OR
Idaho	Ida.	ID	Pennsylvania	Penn.	PA
Illinois	Ill.	IL	Rhode Island	R.I.	RI
Indiana	Ind.	IN	South Carolina	S.C.	SC
Iowa	Ia.	IA	South Dakota	S.Dak.	SD
Kansas	Kans.	KS	Tennessee	Tenn.	TN
Kentucky	Ky.	KY	Texas	Tex.	TX
Louisiana	La.	LA	Utah	Ut.	UT
Maine	Me.	ME	Vermont	Vt.	VT
Maryland	Md.	MD	Virginia	Va.	VA
Massachusetts	Mass.	MA	Washington	Wash.	WA
Michigan	Mich.	MI	West Virginia	W. Va.	WV
Minnesota	Minn.	MN	Wisconsin	Wis.	WI
Mississippi	Miss.	MS	Wyoming	Wyo.	WY
Missouri	Mo.	MO			

Activity B: Draw two envelopes. Address each one by using the information below. First use the old, regular abbreviations. Second, use the newer, two-letter post office abbreviations.

This letter is being sent by Maria Gonzalez. Ms. Gonzalez lives at 202 Adams Street in Detroit, Michigan. Her ZIP code is 48238. The letter is being sent to Rose Chang. Ms. Chang lives at 45 South Elm Place in Houston, Texas. Her ZIP code is 77015.

Summary

Mr. Collins and Wendy had worked through all the steps she needed to know about writing a letter of application. Wendy had gotten all the help that Mr. Collins could give her.

Now Wendy was on her own. She felt sure of herself because she had studied and worked hard.

When she got ready to write a real letter of application, Wendy made a list of the things that Mr. Collins had taught her. She wanted to remember everything she needed to write her letter. Here's her list.

1. Use a correct form for a business letter. The two styles used most often are the full block style and the modified block style.

    a. Full Block Style: All seven parts of the business letter go up against the left-hand margin.

    b. Modified Block Style: The return address, the date, each paragraph, the complimentary close, and the signature are indented.

2. The body of the letter should include all the information requested in the ad. It should also include my telephone number and the times I can be reached.

3. No matter which style of letter I use, the envelope should have the return address in the upper left-hand corner. The address of the person to whom I'm writing should be several lines below that and toward the center. The stamp goes in the upper right-hand corner. (Note: An example of an envelope can be seen on page 35.)

CHAPTER REVIEW

Review Activity A: Number your paper from 1 to 10. If the statement is true, write *True* next to the number of that statement. If it is not true, write *False*.

1. The parts of a business letter are the return address, inside address, salutation, body, and complimentary close.
2. A letter should always include the date on which the letter is written.
3. The salutation is a way of greeting the person to whom you are writing.
4. The body of the letter tells why you are writing.
5. In the full block style letter, everything except the body of the letter lines up at the right-hand margin.
6. The modified block style letter has indented paragraphs.
7. You never have to give references if you don't want to include them.
8. Unless a company asks for your telephone number, don't include it in your letter.
9. When you write a letter of application, it is a good idea to list all of your hobbies.
10. It is necessary to include your name and address on an envelope when you address it.

Review Activity B: Number your paper from 1 to 7. Read the seven parts of a business letter listed below. Rewrite this list in the order in which these parts should appear in a letter.

- body
- date
- return address
- signature
- complimentary close
- inside address
- salutation

Review Activity C: Read this full block style letter. It contains mistakes. It also leaves out important information. Write the numbers of the lines that need to be improved. Describe the mistake in each case. **Clue:** Correct punctuation is important in a business letter.

1.	2517 Bartley Street
2.	Chicago, Ill. 60609
3.	September 12, 1999
4.	Dr. Phillip Moore
5.	12 Arrington Circle
6.	Miami, FL
7.	Dear Dr. Moore
8.	I saw your ad in the <u>Chicago Flash</u> for a
9.	receptionist. I will be moving to Miami next
10.	month. I am interested in applying for the job.
11.	I have worked as a receptionist for a doctor
12.	here in Chicago for four years. I like meeting
13.	and working with people
14.	If you would like an interview, please call me
15.	when I get to Miami.
16.	Love
17.	
18.	Cynthia

Review Activity D: Rewrite the letter in Review Activity C. Correct all errors. Add any information you think is necessary for a good letter of application. When you finish, address an envelope for this letter.

CHAPTER 3

Including a Résumé

Anthony Jackson went to see an employment counselor at his state's employment center. Anthony had not been able to get the type of job he wanted even though he had been trying since he got out of high school three months before.

The counselor interviewed Anthony. She realized that he had many good points in his favor. He had a good school record and had worked part time. His references from his part-time job were excellent. Anthony had a polite manner and seemed to know how to apply for a job both in person and by letter. After Ms. Drake, the counselor, asked more questions, she discovered what the problem was.

"Mr. Jackson, I feel that no employer has gotten a real picture of your ability. I have a feeling that if you had included a *résumé* with your letters or had taken one with you to the interview, you would have gotten a job before now. This short account of your career and qualifications could have been used when you applied for a job."

"Why would a résumé have helped me?" asked Anthony.

"Well, only so many facts can or should be told in a letter of application. A résumé gives a clearer picture of you and your qualifications. It gives you a chance to tell the employer much information in an easy-to-read style," explained Ms. Drake.

"I learned to write a résumé in high school. I'm sure that if I went back and looked over my notes, I could write a good description of my skills. Ms. Drake, after I write my résumé, would you be willing to look it over and tell me what you think of it?" Anthony asked.

"Of course I would. As soon as you have finished a rough draft, call and make an appointment to see me. I'll be happy to look over your résumé."

Anthony went home and found the notes he had kept from high school.

Lesson 1: Advantages of Submitting a Résumé

The first thing Anthony found among his notes was a list of reasons why a person should submit a résumé with every job application. Let's take a look at this list on pages 43 and 44.

1. A résumé gives you a chance to present yourself in a good manner.
2. You can give more information about yourself in a résumé than it is possible to give in a letter or even on some applications.
3. A good résumé will show an employer how well you can organize information.

4. A résumé tells the employer that you really care about getting the job because you have taken the time and the trouble to write a résumé.

The four points on that list made sense to Anthony. He remembered coming away from job interviews and completing application forms. He had often thought, "I wish they'd asked me about my attendance record at school or if I got good grades in math." He had often wished he could tell other information about himself to an employer, but he was never asked.

Activity A: Follow these steps to begin creating your résumé.

Put your mind to work. What might you want to include in your résumé? Think of some of the good things about yourself that you would like an employer to know. Have you had other jobs? Did you do well in certain subjects in school? Have you won any awards? Are there some *business machines* that you know how to operate? For example, have you ever used a photocopy machine, a personal computer, or a 10-key calculator? What person could you list as a reference?

Now, on a sheet of paper, jot down everything you can think of that you would like to include in your résumé. Remember that relatives are not good choices for references. The employer is going to think that such people will say nice things about you just because you are related to them. Instead, you can list as references people for whom you have worked. You can also list clergymen, coaches, club moderators, teachers, and other adults who know you well. The people you list as references should be able to describe your character, how well you do things, and how well you get along with others.

Lesson 2: What to Include in a Résumé

As Anthony looked over his notes, he realized that he would have to review them carefully. A résumé has several parts, and it is important to remember each one. It is also important to remember what goes into each part. Let's take a moment and review with Anthony.

The résumé should include the following parts.

- Personal information
- Career goals and aims
- Education
- Employment experience
- Extracurricular and community activities
- Awards and honors
- References

The arrangement or *order* of these parts should be decided by your age, your experience, and the job for which you are applying. Generally, the most important items are listed first in a résumé.

Although you are not required to give your age on a résumé, your age is a factor in what you have done and what you are prepared to do. A young person just graduating from high school would list extracurricular activities in which he or she participated in school. If you are a person who has been out of high school for a time, you would probably not mention that information. Instead you might list community groups in which you are active.

If you are just out of high school, you may have little or no employment experience. You would want to put other sections first in your résumé. A person who has had several jobs before applying for this one will want to put the experience section near the top of his or her résumé to show that he or she is prepared for this new job. Career goals would also probably differ depending on your age and experience.

Activity A: This activity will review arranging information in a résumé. Fifteen words are missing from this exercise. Number your paper from 1 to 15. Write the correct missing word next to each number. Use the words listed in the box to help you. Only one word goes on each line.

employment	references	goals
experience	order	community
graduated	aims	age
seven	information	applying
résumé	end	experience

There are 1) _____ parts to a résumé. These parts include the following: personal 2) _____ , career 3) _____ and 4) _____ , education, employment 5) _____ , extracurricular and/or community activities, awards and honors, and 6) _____ .

No definite 7) _____ must be used when writing a résumé. The order should be decided by your 8) _____ , your 9) _____ , and the job for which you are 10) _____

Extracurricular activities would be important for someone who has just 11) _____ from high school. For people who have been out of high school for a while, it would be better to list 12) _____ activities.

A person who has had no job experience either would not put the 13) _____ section in the résumé at all or else would put this section near the 14) _____ of his or her résumé. Someone who has previous job experience would probably list this information near the beginning of the 15) _____ .

Personal Information

Personal information includes your name, address, and telephone number. Be sure to include your ZIP code with your address. Include your area code with your telephone number.

Career Goals and Aims

What is your goal in business? Word your *career goals* and aims to indicate the specific type of job that you want. Make these goals broad so that you can be considered for more than one job. For example, if you are looking for a job as a plumbing trainee or apprentice, your long-range goal might be "to become a master plumber." This aim might take you many years to achieve, but it is a career goal toward which you are working.

Education

For someone who has recently graduated from school, this section on education can be especially important on your résumé. Be sure to include special courses you have taken that relate to the job you are seeking. You should also mention areas or courses in which you got good grades.

Employment Experience

Work experience should include all full-time and part-time jobs that you have had. It should also include any job you performed as a volunteer. Babysitting, snow shoveling, lawn mowing, and other similar jobs done for neighbors and friends should also be included. Such experience will show that you are responsible and dependable.

Extracurricular and/or Community Activities; Awards and Honors

Recent high school graduates should include any *extracurricular* activity outside the regular school curriculum. Examples might include sports teams, school newspaper, debating club, plays or musicals, etc. All applicants should also include any community groups or activities in which they participated. You might indicate offices held, specific duties performed, or awards earned. People that are active and responsible in clubs and organizations are often hardworking and dependable on the job as well.

References

An employer likes to be able to talk to other people to find out how good they think you will be at a job. Include at least three *references* in your résumé. You can use teachers, previous employers, family friends, or clergymen. Do **not** use a member of your family. Always ask people if they are willing to give a reference for you before you list their name in a résumé. People listed as references should be able to describe your character and to tell how well you do things and how well you get along with others.

Activity B: Draw a chart on your paper like the one given below. On the next page is a list of information about Anthony Jackson. Read each item. Then write the number of each item in the correct column on your chart.

Personal Information	Goals	Education	Experience	Extracurricular/ Community Activities

Information About Anthony Jackson

1. Wants to be a licensed automobile mechanic
2. Sang in the church choir
3. Graduated from high school
4. Worked part time in a gas station
5. Lives at 511 North Marine Street
6. Took a course in auto mechanics at night school
7. Worked on community block party committee
8. Has helped neighbors fix their cars
9. Would like to own his own auto repair shop
10. Took auto mechanics course in high school
11. Lives in Walla Walla, Washington
12. Was senior class president
13. Served as representative to high school's student government association
14. Does repairs on small appliances for neighbors
15. Has the following telephone number: (509) 555-7760

Lesson 3: Sample Résumés

Anthony Jackson completed a list of information for his résumé. He listed personal information plus facts about his career goals, education, experience, extracurricular or community activities, and references. Then he was ready to write the first version or *draft* of his résumé. A copy of the résumé that Anthony wrote is shown on the next page.

Read this résumé carefully. Find the main parts in this résumé. Notice the information that is included in each part. Be prepared to answer questions about Anthony's résumé after you have studied it.

Anthony J. Jackson
511 North Marine Street
Walla Walla, Washington 98511
(509) 555-7760

CAREER GOALS
- To be a licensed automobile mechanic
- To own my own auto repair shop

EDUCATION
Graduated from Northwest High School, June, 1998
Majored in auto mechanics
Received best grades in math, science, and auto mechanics (A's)
Completed night school course in auto mechanics at Adult Night
    Center, June, 1999

EXTRACURRICULAR ACTIVITIES
President of Senior Class
Representative to student government
Member of Northwest Choir

EXPERIENCE
Worked part time at Hal's Service Station for two years
Helped neighbors with car repairs
Repaired small appliances for neighbors

REFERENCES
Mr. Hal Penn, Owner   Mr. William Turner
Hal's Service Station   Auto Mechanics Teacher
11 Pacific Highway   Northwest High School
Walla Walla, Washington 98503   Walla Walla, Washington 98513
(509) 555-1742   (509) 555-6756

Mrs. Irma Newcome, Neighbor
515 North Marine Street
Walla Walla, Washington 98511
(509) 555-9443

Activity A: On a sheet of paper, number from 1 to 10. Then answer these questions about Anthony Jackson's résumé.

1. What education did Anthony list that relates to the job of automobile mechanic?

2. Why would an employer be impressed by the extracurricular activities in which Anthony took part?

3. Which two of Anthony's work experiences relate most directly to the job of auto mechanic?

4. Why is Mr. William Turner a good reference if Anthony is applying for the job of auto mechanic?

5. Mrs. Newsome is one of the neighbors for whom Anthony has done car repairs and small appliance repairs. Is she a good person for him to use as a reference? Why?

6. Why do you think an employer would be especially impressed by Anthony's going to night school?

7. Mr. Hal Penn seems like a good reference. Why?

8. How do Anthony's career goals relate to the job of mechanic's assistant?

9. If you were thinking of hiring Anthony, which reference would you call first? Why?

10. What questions would you ask Mr. Penn or Mr. Turner to get information that is not included in the résumé?

A Résumé for the Experienced Person

Among his high school notes, Anthony found a sample résumé for an experienced job applicant. He couldn't use that sample to help him with his own résumé, so he lent it to Norman Flynn, a neighbor.

Mr. Flynn was thirty years old and was looking for another job. He knew something about writing résumés, but he had not written one since he graduated from high school. That old one would be no good to him now. First, the information in it was out of date. Second, he had gained more work experience. He wanted to change the order of his résumé and to include some things that happened after that old résumé had been written. Let's take a look at the new résumé that Mr. Flynn wrote.

Norman H. Flynn
510 North Marine Street
Walla Walla, Washington 98511
(509) 555-2233

CAREER GOALS
- To be head bookkeeper for a large corporation
- To continue in that job until retirement

EXPERIENCE
1990 to Present: Assistant bookkeeper
                    Elgin's Department Store
                    Walla Walla, Washington 98546
1986 to 1990:   Bookkeeper trainee
                    Link's Hardware Stores
                    Walla Walla, Washington 98530
1988 to Present: Income tax consultant, part-time position
                    Fill out income tax forms for 20 clients in spare time

COMMUNITY ACTIVITIES
Treasurer: Church of St. Jude, 1990 to present
Treasurer and Business Manager: Walla Walla Little League, 1987
               to present
Member: South Shores Community Group
Volunteer: Keep gift shop books for South Shores General Hospital

EDUCATION
Graduated from South Shores High, June, 1986
Completed undergraduate courses at Washington University
               bookkeeping, accounting, business organization, and
               computers

REFERENCES   Mr. Arthur Day
               Present Employer
               Elgin's Department Store
               Walla Walla, Washington 98546
               (509) 555-6983

               Rev. Julius Fitzhughes
               Pastor
               Church of St. Jude
               7819 Wells Avenue
               Walla Walla, Washington 98511
               (509) 555-4635

               Mr. Felix Wist
               President
               South Shores General Hospital Volunteers
               44 Hospital Road
               Walla Walla, Washington 98545
               (509) 555-1297

How Mr. Flynn's Résumé Is Different

Notice the differences between the résumé Anthony Jackson wrote and the one Mr. Flynn wrote. They are both good for the purpose intended. They are both suited to the age and experience of that particular person.

The information in these two résumés is arranged differently. Some important differences can be seen in the employment section and in the references section. Notice the specific information that Mr. Flynn included in these two parts of his résumé.

Employment Experience
Mr. Flynn listed his work experience second in his résumé because he felt that information about him would most interest an employer. He put community activities next because his activities in his community relate to the kind of work for which he is looking.

References
Notice what a good selection of references Mr. Flynn made. First, he listed the man he now works for. That is a very impressive choice. A prospective employer would know that Mr. Flynn is being very open about the job he is presently doing.

Then, Mr. Flynn listed the pastor of his church. The pastor can tell an employer about Mr. Flynn's character and also about the *volunteer* work he does as church treasurer.

Finally, he listed the president of the volunteer group to which he belongs. This person can tell about the time Mr. Flynn spends as a volunteer and about how he keeps the books for this organization.

Lesson 4: Checklists for Résumés

Anthony found among his papers a list of capitalization, punctuation, and spelling rules. The list was marked by a large title that said, "YOUR RÉSUMÉ MUST BE PERFECT."

Anthony was glad that he found that list. It reminded him of the little things that can be so important when an employer looks at a résumé.

1. When writing an address, put a comma between the city and state. Put no punctuation between the state and the ZIP code.

2. When writing a telephone number, put the area code in parentheses. Put a hyphen after the first three numbers of the telephone number.

3. Capital letters must be used for the first letter of all people's names, street names, cities, states, businesses, schools, etc.

4. All words should be spelled correctly.

Activity A: Listed below are ten items that you might find on a résumé. Some items have errors in them. On a sheet of paper, correct the items that have errors. (There are 12 errors.)

1. Oklahoma City, Oklahoma, 73125
2. Mr. John A fisher, Manager
3. 2634 Green Strete
4. Mark Twain senior High school
5. February 14 1958
6. Mrs. charlotte Best, Teacher
7. 301/555/4736
8. Bill's Discount store
9. Pennsylvania University
10. Dr Sylvia Greer

Activity B: This list of items could be included in résumés. On your own paper, list those things that you would pick for your résumé.

- perfect attendance award two years in a row
- experience working at a full-time or part-time job
- activities in which you have participated at your church
- community groups to which you have belonged
- special courses you took in high school

Activity C: Now you are ready to write your own résumé. Use the list you made in Activity A, page 44, to help you. Review the sample résumés. As you write your rough draft, use this *checklist.*

Résumé Checklist

1. Have I decided on the organization that will suit my age and my experience best?
2. Have I worded my goals and aims so that they are geared to the job that I am trying to get?
3. Have I listed all of my education? Have I emphasized the things I did well? Have I emphasized courses related to the job I want?
4. If I have work experience, have I listed the specific skills and duties related to the job I am trying to get?
5. Have I listed extracurricular activities or community activities that reflect my interest in the area?
6. Have I selected the most impressive references from different people who know me well?
7. Is my résumé spaced well? Will it have an attractive, neat appearance when it is finished?
8. Are the headings clear? Do they stand out from other information?
9. Is all my information correct? Have all typing errors been corrected? Have all spelling, capitalization, and punctuation errors been corrected? Is my résumé perfect?

10. Have I used no more than two pages?
11. Is my wording consistent?
12. Have I used the suggestions in this chapter and the checklist to help me write my résumé?

Summary

A résumé is important to help you get a job. It allows you to present more information about yourself than you can include in a letter. It gives the employer a better idea of what you can do.

A résumé should include personal information, career goals, your educational background, your employment background, something about the extracurricular or community activities in which you have participated, awards and honors you have received, and the names of people whom you are using as references. How you arrange this information depends on your age, the amount of experience you have had, and what you consider most important for the employer to know.

Probably the most important thing for you to remember about a résumé is that it should be perfect. It should be free of all errors in capitalization, punctuation, and spelling. All information you have included should be correct; for example, names, addresses, ZIP codes, and telephone numbers.

A good résumé can make all the difference between being unemployed and getting a job.

CHAPTER REVIEW

Review Activity A: Match each term in the first column with its description in the second column.

Term

1. personal information
2. career goals and aims
3. education
4. employment experience
5. extracurricular and community activities
6. awards and honors
7. references

Description

a. all full-time and part-time jobs you had
b. the names, addresses, and phone numbers of people who can describe your ability to do the job
c. what schools you graduated from; what courses you have taken
d. your name, address, and telephone number
e. extra clubs you joined in school; organizations you have joined in your community
f. special recognitions of your achievements
g. what you hope to be doing in the future

Review Activity B: Label each sentence as *True* or *False*.

1. A recent high school graduate will probably want to list work experience before education.
2. The order of the items in a résumé should depend upon the job for which the person wants to be hired.
3. You may leave your address and phone number out of your résumé.
4. An experienced person will probably want to list work experiences near the beginning of the résumé.
5. You can use your mother and father as references.

Review Activity C: Part of a résumé is shown below. It contains errors in spelling, capitalization, and punctuation. On a sheet of paper, rewrite this part of the résumé. Make all necessary corrections.

---

willaim t rogers
1758 maple streat
philadelphia pennsylvania, 19032
215 555 8493

referances
    mr john dilland owner
    dilland corner store
    788 cherry lane
    philadelphia pennsylvania 19024
    215/555/4466

eduction
    gradated from central high school, june 1987
    took courses in english and math at pennsylvania state
    college

Review Activity D: Answer these questions on your own paper.

1. Why is it a good idea to include a résumé in a letter of application?
2. What are the main parts of a résumé?
3. How would you decide the order to be used in your résumé?
4. What kind of information should you include in the section for extra-curricular or community activities?
5. Should you include as a reference a boss with whom you could not get along? Why or why not?

CHAPTER 4

Filling Out the Application

Laura Smith worked as a clerk-typist in the personnel department of Caine Supply Company. Every day she saw people come in to apply for jobs, and every day she saw some of their *job applications* thrown into the wastebasket.

Because this puzzled her, she asked her *supervisor*, "Why do so many job applications get thrown out?"

"We don't bother with applications that are not filled out correctly. We look the application over. If it has mistakes or if all the information is not given, into the wastebasket it goes," explained the supervisor.

"Why are mistakes or incomplete information so important?" asked Laura.

"A job application is probably one of the most important things a person ever fills out. If people don't care enough to make it perfect, how are they going to be when they start working? We think they'll be sloppy and careless. We don't want people like that working for us," said the supervisor.

Laura thought about what the supervisor said. She certainly could see why the store would not hire people who did not turn in a perfect application. She remembered the care she had taken to get her application right, and now she was glad she had.

A few weeks after Laura's talk with her supervisor, Laura's younger brother, Steve, graduated from high school. He was ready to look for a job. Laura told him about what her supervisor said and warned him to do a good job on his job applications. After several weeks went by and Steve had still not gotten a job, Laura asked him why he was having trouble.

"I don't know, Sis," said Steve. "I'm not having any luck. I bet I've filled out twenty applications, and no job. I've got another application here that I'm turning in this afternoon."

"Let me take a look at it," said Laura.

She studied the application for a few minutes, looked at her brother, and shook her head. "No wonder you're not getting a job. This application looks awful. You've made mistakes, left out information, and made sloppy erasures. I wouldn't hire you either if I didn't know you and looked at these pages. An employer judges you by your application. The employer usually sees your application first. If he or she likes it, you may be called in for an interview."

Lesson 1: The Fact Sheet

"Okay, Sis, I guess I need your help," replied Steve.

"First," said Laura, "you need to prepare a *fact sheet* with all the information you have to put on an application. The fact sheet can be taken with you when you go to apply for a job. You can use it if you need to fill out the application at the company where you are applying for a job. Even if you can bring the application home, you can refer to the fact sheet instead of having to look up the information every time you need it."

"What would I put on a fact sheet?" asked Steve.

"Well, what are some of the things you've had to put on an application?" questioned Laura.

"You mean things like my *Social Security number* and my *school records?"* asked Steve.

"Right," said Laura. "I have my fact sheet right upstairs. I'll go get it, and you can use it as a sample to help you write yours."

The fact sheet sample that Laura gave Steve to use is shown on the next page. It contains all the important information that Laura had to supply when she was job hunting.

Read Laura's fact sheet carefully. What major parts are included in this fact sheet?

Social Security #777-38-0976

EDUCATION

John Murphy Senior High
1600 McNair Avenue
Topeka, Kansas 66656

Course: Business
Years attended: 4
Graduated: June 2, 1990

Topeka Community College
203 South Plains Road
Topeka, Kansas 66623

Course: Computer
   Programming
Years attended: 2
Graduated: June 4, 1992
Degree: Associate of Arts

EXPERIENCE

1990 to present:
Caine Supply Company
1543 Travis Street
Topeka, Kansas 66609
(913) 555-1758

Position: Clerk-Typist
Supervisor: Timothy Clark
Reason for leaving: To get job
   as computer programmer

REFERENCES

Ms. Amelia Carter
Business Education Teacher
John Murphy Senior High
(See above for address)
(913) 555-0770

Ms. Lillian Newly
Programming Instructor
Topeka Community College
(See above for address)
(913) 555-9063

Mr. Timothy Clark, President
Caine Supply Company
(See above for address)
(913) 555-7718

As Steve looked over Laura's fact sheet, he could see why she included what she did. He remembered that when he was filling out an application one day, he was so nervous that he forgot his Social Security number. He didn't have it with him, so he left that space blank. He also remembered not being sure how long he had worked at the part-time job he had while he was in high school. He wasn't always sure he knew how to spell names correctly.

Laura gave him a good piece of advice. If you don't remember how to spell people's names, call and ask. They won't mind. If you are not sure how to spell street or business names, look them up in the telephone book and check the spelling.

Activity A: Listed on pages 64 and 65 are ten facts about a person. On your own paper, write *Yes* for the items that should be included on a fact sheet. Write *No* for the items that would not be included.

1. The full name of the high school the person attended
2. The person's Social Security number
3. The number of basketball games in which that person scored more than five points
4. The name of a teacher who was very nice to the person but who had never taught the person
5. The address and ZIP code of the high school that the person attended
6. The name and address of that person's Aunt Sue to serve as a reference
7. The name of the company where that person works

8. The name and address of the math teacher the person had last year (as a reference)

9. The name of the principal of the person's school (as a reference)

10. The reason the person wants to leave his or her present job

Activity B: Write a fact sheet for your own use. Include all of the information that Laura included on her fact sheet. If you are not sure of the spelling of any words, check them. Use the hints that Laura gave Steve.

Updating Your Fact Sheet

It is important to remember that you cannot use the same fact sheet for years and years. You may want to include other jobs you have had or any additional education. Each time you apply for a job, check your fact sheet to make sure that the information on it is current. If it isn't, update your fact sheet by adding whatever does not appear on it.

Activity C: On your own paper, list the names of six people that you could use as references. Write their names, spelled correctly. Then write their addresses and phone numbers.

Remember: You do not want to use the name of a relative as a reference.

Lesson 2: Application Vocabulary

As Laura looked over Steve's application, she realized that there were some words whose meanings Steve might not know. She knew that before he could fill out an application correctly, he would have to be sure of the meanings of those words. She offered to give him some help.

Laura gave Steve a glossary of terms that he might find on an application. A glossary is like a little dictionary. Here is a copy of the glossary that Laura gave Steve.

Application Glossary

Address   — The place where you live, where your references can be reached, or where your school or employer is located. An address should include the number and street name, the city and state, and the ZIP code. Remember that a comma goes between the city and state, but no comma is used between the state and the ZIP code.

College   — The name of the college or university you attended. You do not have to graduate to include it.

Company — The place where you work, or places where you have worked before.

Course   — The subject in which you majored in school. In high school you might have taken an academic, a college preparatory, a business, an auto mechanics, or a general course.

Degree — An award offered if you graduated from a community or regular four-year college. You might earn an Associate of Arts, Bachelor of Arts, or Bachelor of Science. These degrees are usually written as A.A., B.A., and B.S.

Experience — A term referring to other jobs that you have held. This section of the application may also ask for the dates worked at this job, the name of the company, the address of the company, your duties and title, the name of your direct supervisor, and the reason why you left the job.

Position — Job or job title, such as clerk-typist or receptionist.

References — The names, positions, addresses, and sometimes the telephone numbers of people who know you and can talk about the kind of person you are. They might tell how well you do things and how well you get along with others. References can include people for whom you have worked, friends, teachers, or clergymen.

Signature — A handwritten (rather than typed or printed) name; most applications require that you write, not print, your name somewhere near the bottom of the application.

Study this glossary carefully. Understanding the meanings of these words will help you to do a good job on filling out your application.

Activity A: Number from 1 to 9 on your own paper. Choose the correct vocabulary word to complete each sentence. Write the word next to its matching number. Use the words listed in the box below to help you.

references	position	signature
course	address	college
company	degree	experience

1. Wherever you are asked to give an _____ , you should write the complete information including the ZIP code.

2. An application may ask what _____ you took in high school.

3. The application may also ask if you went to _____ .

4. If you graduated from college, you may have to add what _____ you received when you graduated.

5. Any work you did at jobs before the one you are applying for is called _____ .

6. You may have to give the name of the _____ for whom you worked.

7. You may also have to say what _____ you are applying for.

8. You will probably have to give names, addresses, or telephone numbers of people who know you. These names are called _____ .

9. Near the end of the application, you will have to write your _____ .

Activity B: Number your paper from 1 to 9. Read the words in the first column. Next to each number, write the letter of the correct explanation from the second column.

Word

1. signature
2. address
3. company
4. references
5. college
6. course
7. position
8. degree
9. experience

Explanation

a. should include the number of the house or building and the name of the street, city, state, and ZIP code
b. should be the name of the college you went to
c. the name of the place where you worked
d. what you majored in
e. what you get when you graduate from college
f. other jobs you have held
g. names of people who can say what kind of person you are and what kind of work you do
h. your written name
i. job

Lesson 3: Avoiding Errors

"Some items on applications," Laura explained to Steve, "are not hard to read. But they can be tricky to figure out. It takes some experience to understand what information they want. For example, many applications ask for the *place of birth.* That doesn't mean the name of the hospital where you were born. It means the city and state where you were born. If you were born in another country, you would write that name."

Laura handed Steve a sheet of paper. "Here are other tricky things you may find on applications. Study this list carefully," Laura said. "You may want to take it with you when you apply for a job. If you don't have to fill the application out at the place where you apply, you will want to keep it handy at home. You can refer to it as you fill out the application."

Tricky Application Items

"Position applied for"
  The job or jobs you are trying to get

"List last or present employer first"
  On most applications you are asked to list your employment record starting with the last job you had or the job you have at the time you apply. You then list the job before that, and the job before that, and so on, until you list your very first job last. That section of an application may look like this:

| 1996 to Present | Miller Supply Company
1100 Grant Street
Boston, MA 02109 |
| 1993 to 1996 | Homing Graphics
1567 Sober Avenue
Boston, MA 02110 |
| 1991 to 1993 | Grass Roots Garage
100 Main Street
Sturbridge, MA 01566 |

"Reason for leaving"
  You should give the reason why you left a job. Your reason might be that you learned new skills or changed careers, the company went out of business, or you were laid off.

"May we call your present employer?"
 You may not care to have the person for whom you are presently working know that you are looking for another job. It is your right to answer this question, "No."

"References"
 If an application has three spaces for references, give three references. If it has two spaces, give two. Make sure you give whatever number of references the application requires.

Activity A: Listed below are five items from an application. Number from 1 to 5 on your paper. Match each item with the section of the application to which it belongs. Write the correct name of the item in each case.

1. I wanted to try a new kind of work.

2. Mary Smith, Typing Teacher   Rev. James Deems, Pastor
    Durant High School   Calvary Baptist Church
    8763 Clyde Boulevard   11 Thames Avenue
    Salt Lake City, Utah 84154   Salt Lake City, Utah 84111
    (801) 555-7463   (801) 555-1146

3. Waiter

4. Yes

5. 1998 to Present   Fisher's Eatery
                         665 Laird Street
                         Salt Lake City, Utah 84123

    1996 to 1998   Hank's Pizza Parlor
                         2749 Flame Road
                         Salt Lake City, Utah 84101

Lesson 4: Interpreting Application Forms

As Steve continued to apply for jobs, he found that some of the applications were harder to understand. He went to Laura and asked for more help.

Steve was smart. He made a list of the things he found on applications that were hard to understand. Laura took the list and made him the guide sheet below. Steve studied it carefully.

Application Guide

"Kind of work desired"—means "What kind of job would you like to have?"

"Have you ever been employed by this company?"—means "Did you ever work before for this company?"

"Have you ever been employed by a similar concern?"—means "Did you ever work for a company that makes the same kind of product or offers the same kind of service as this company?"

"Is all the information on this application true? If we discover that it is not, that will be considered sufficient cause for dismissal."—means "If our company hires you and then finds out you did not tell the truth on your application, you could be fired."

"In case of emergency, notify"—means "If you have an accident or get sick, whom should we call?"

"Final rate of pay"—means "before you left that job, how much were you being paid?" (Refers to job you had before)

"Nature of work done"—means "What kind of work did you do on this job?" (Refers to job you had before)

After Steve had studied the application guide, Laura warned him, "Steve, there is no way you can be prepared for every question you will find on every application. If you don't understand something, ask the person who gave you the application. Asking questions can even make a good impression because it tells the person that you really care about doing a good job on the application."

Activity A: Listed below are seven items that might be hard to understand on some applications. Answer each item. Use the "Possible Answers" listed in the box. Use each answer once.

Possible Answers		
Mary Smith, mother	$4.50 per hour	No
Clerk-typist	Yes, Smith & Sons	Yes
Filed and ran errands		

1. Kind of work desired?
2. Have you ever been employed by this company?
3. Nature of work done?
4. In case of emergency, notify:
5. Is all the information on this application true?
6. Have you ever been employed by a similar concern?
7. Final rate of pay?

Activity B: Suppose you were fired from your last job because you did not come to work regularly. What would you say on an application for a new job about your reason for leaving your last job? Would you tell the truth? Suppose there were good reasons why you did not come to work regularly. Write a short paragraph explaining what you would say on the application.

Lesson 5: An Application Checklist

When you begin to fill out an application, you should remember to do seven things. When you finish, check your application to make sure that you have done all seven things correctly.

1. Follow all directions. If you are asked to type your application, type it. Otherwise, always use a pen.

2. If you are asked to print, print the information. Use capital letters where appropriate and lowercase letters otherwise. See the example below:

Smith	*Steve*	*J.*
(PRINT) Last name	First name	Middle Initial

3. Make sure you fill in **all** blanks. If something does not apply to you, put N/A (for Not Applicable) on the blank line.

4. Make sure your application is neat and easy to read. Try not to erase. If you must erase, be as neat as possible.
   Hint: You might use an erasable pen or correction fluid.

5. Make sure all the information that you give is correct. Use your fact sheet whenever necessary. Check and make sure that you have the correct spelling of the names of people, streets, cities, and states. Make sure that the street numbers, ZIP codes, and telephone numbers are correct.

6. Make sure you have been honest about all the information that you have given.

7. If possible, get someone else to check your application after you have checked it.

Activity A: Number your paper from 1 to 10. If the statement is true, write *True* next to the number. If the statement is not true, write *False* next to the number.

1. A job application should be as perfect as you can make it.

2. If an application says that it should be typed, you may fill it out with a pen.

3. If something on an application does not apply to you, leave that section blank.

4. Some employers think that people who turn in messy applications will be messy workers.

5. A fact sheet is given to the employer.

6. You can use the same fact sheet for years.

7. Make sure that you use capital letters where appropriate.

8. It is a good idea to fill in an application with a pencil.

9. Check the spelling on your application.

10. It is a poor idea to ask someone else to check your application for you.

Summary

A completed application says something about the kind of person you are. The better the application looks and the more accurate it is, the more likely you are to get the job. You must be honest about the information you give on an application. Some companies will fire you if they find out that what you wrote on your application is not true.

CHAPTER REVIEW

Review Activity A: Write short answers to the ten questions below.

1. What are two reasons for preparing a fact sheet before you apply for a job?
2. What three kinds of information should you include in your fact sheet?
3. Why is it a good idea to include in the fact sheet information that you know by heart?
4. If you are not sure how to spell a person's name, what can you do?
5. If you are not sure how to spell a street name or the name of a company, what can you do?
6. Why is it important to update your fact sheet every time you apply for a new job?
7. What seven things should you check when filling out an application?
8. Why is it important to turn in a perfect application?
9. If your application is incomplete or messy, what might an employer think of you?
10. When is it all right to erase on an application?

Review Activity B: Number your paper from 1 to 9. Then write a word from the word box for each explanation on pages 76 and 77.

address	company	college
course	position	references
degree	signature	experience

1. Your written name
2. Job

3. What you majored in in high school or college
4. Your street address, city, state, and ZIP code
5. What you got when you graduated from college
6. Name of the college you attended
7. Names of people who can describe what kind of person you are and what kind of work you can do
8. Other jobs you have held
9. Name of the place you worked for

Review Activity C: Number your paper from 1 to 9. Choose the correct answer from the word box to complete each statement. Write the correct answer next to each number.

directions	type	neat	capital
looks good	pencil	N/A	lowercase
Not Applicable	blanks		

1. You should follow all _____ on an application.
2. If they ask you to _____ , you should type.
3. Never use a _____ when you fill out an application.
4. When you print, you should use _____ letters where appropriate.
5. Use _____ letters everywhere else.
6. Make sure you fill in all _____ .
7. If something does not apply to you, put _____ or _____ on the blank line.
8. Make sure your application _____ and is easy to read.
9. If you must erase, be as _____ as possible.

Review Activity D: The following items might appear on a job application. Write the information you would supply for each item. Use your own paper.

Hint: Some items may not apply to you if you have never worked before. What do you write when something doesn't apply to you?

1. Place of birth
2. Job applied for or position applied for
3. List last or present employer first
4. Final rate of pay
5. Nature of work done
6. Reason for leaving
7. May we call your present employer?
8. List three references
9. Kind of work desired
10. Have you ever been employed by this company?
11. Is all the information on this application true?
12. In case of emergency, notify...

Review Activity E: Copy this application checklist. Keep it handy so that you can refer to it whenever you need it.

1. Did I follow all the directions on the application?
2. If I printed, did I use capital letters where I should have?
3. Did I fill in all the blanks?
4. Is my application neat and easy to read?
5. Have I checked my application to make sure that all information I included was correct?
6. Was all the information I gave honest?
7. Did I get someone else to check my application after I checked it?

CHAPTER 5

Applying by Phone

The telephone rang in the *personnel* division of Hilbert Electronics. This big, important company hired many people. Cynthia Dawson picked up the phone and said, "Good morning. Personnel division, Hilbert Electronics. May I help you?"

"Yeah," said the voice at the other end. "I want a job."

Cynthia sighed to herself and thought, "Here we go again." "What job are you interested in?" she asked, politely.

"This here job you got advertised," was the reply.

"Ma'am, we have twelve jobs advertised. Could you tell me which one you mean?" Cynthia asked.

"Yeah, the one for a stock clerk," the woman answered.

"Was that stock clerk position for the supply warehouse or for the docks?" Cynthia inquired.

And so the conversation went. After about fifteen minutes, Cynthia hung up the phone. Then she turned to her friend Ruth and said, "I am sick and tired of talking to people on the phone who don't have the slightest idea how to make a call, especially a call applying for a job. Sometimes I wish I could just hang up on them, but that would be rude."

Ruth laughed. "I know just what you mean," she said. "Sometimes I think we could make a fortune if we wrote a handbook about how to apply for a job on the telephone."

"What a good idea!" exclaimed Cynthia. "Let's write a handbook. We could send it out to people who call us to apply for jobs and who don't seem to know what they are doing. They might not get a job here, but the handbook would help them. They wouldn't sound so bad to the next place they called. I don't care whether we make any money from it. I'd just like to do something to help."

"The first thing I'd put in the handbook would be something about having the information you need before you make the call," said Ruth.

"Right," said Cynthia. "Let's list what you need."

Lesson 1: Be Prepared to Apply by Phone

Ruth and Cynthia started to make a list of the information a person should have handy before he or she calls to apply for a job. Their list looked like the one shown on the next page.

Information
1. Job advertised—exact description
2. Where and when advertised—name of newspaper, job advertisement, date on newspaper or announcement, etc.
3. Fact sheet—information about education and work
4. Days and times when you are available—to go for interview, to complete application, or both
5. Telephone number where you can be reached—if a call back is necessary
6. You should also have paper and pencil to write any information given you during the call. For example, write the date, time, and place for a *job interview* with a prospective employer.
7. It might help to cut the ad and have it with you when you call.

It was clear to Cynthia and Ruth that you have to do some work before you ever dial the telephone number to apply for a job. You will make a much better impression if you have the information at hand. The person who talks with you on the telephone will be impressed by how well-organized you are. It will appear that if you are organized when you call about the job, you will probably be well-organized on the job. You want to make your first contact a good one.

Activity A: Answer these questions on a separate sheet of paper.

1. Why it is necessary to tell the exact job for which you are applying?
2. How will a fact sheet help you during a phone call to apply for a job?
3. Why is it helpful to tell where and when you saw the job advertised?
4. If you are asked when you can come in for an interview, why is it important to be able to answer immediately and accurately?
5. Why should you give a telephone number where you can be reached?
6. Why will you give a better impression if you have all the information you need ready to give when asked?

Activity B: Read the job advertisement given below. It appeared in the *Pittsfield Chronicle* on November 23. Suppose that you were going to answer this ad. On a separate sheet of paper, list the information you would need before you make your call. Be sure to refer to Ruth and Cynthia's list.

> STOCK CLERK to work in supply warehouse. No exp. nec. Should be good in arith. Call Mr. Neal at 555-0800.

Lesson 2: Starting Out Right

"What do you think ought to come next?" Cynthia asked Ruth.

"Well, one of the things I hear from the bosses here in the personnel division is that people don't identify themselves. The other thing they get annoyed about is that it takes some people a long time to get around to saying why they are calling," answered Ruth.

"You're right!" exclaimed Cynthia. "Those are the two complaints I hear, too."

Cynthia and Ruth decided that they would come up with two easy-to-understand rules about making phone calls in answer to job ads. They thought about it for a long time. Finally they decided on the two rules below. Read them carefully to see if you understand them. Would you know what to do first when you make your call?

Rule 1: In a clear, distinct voice, give your first and last name.
Rule 2: Then say why you are calling.
      (For example, "I am calling in answer to your ad for a stock clerk that appeared in Sunday's *News.*")

"That's fine, but we need to tell them what to do when they reach a *central telephone switchboard* like the one we have here," said Cynthia.

"Let's add a third rule," suggested Ruth. "Here it is."

Rule 3: If the *operator* asks you to hold or says that you will be transferred to another person, wait. When the second person comes on the line, repeat the steps in Rules 1 and 2.

Activity A: Imagine that you are telephoning to answer the ad given below. With a classmate or friend, practice making your telephone call. Use the three rules that Cynthia and Ruth wrote. Do not go any further than Rule 3.

> STOCK CLERK wanted for dock warehouse. No exp. nec. Call Mr. Livingstone, 555-7463.

When you practice, use the three different situations described below.
1. Mr. Livingstone is the person who answers when you phone.
2. Mr. Livingstone's secretary answers when you phone.
3. The switchboard operator answers when you phone. She transfers you to the personnel division. Someone in the personnel division transfers you to Mr. Livingstone's secretary, who transfers you to Mr. Livingstone.

Activity B: Call a friend or relative. Ask the person to listen to your voice. Ask him or her to tell you if your voice is clear and easy to understand. Make a list of what this person tells you about your telephone voice.

Lesson 3: Getting and Giving Information

Cynthia and Ruth realized that once a person begins a telephone interview, it is hard to know what may be said. However, they did think that some general rules might help people. The first thing they wanted people to remember was that they should try to make a *good impression*. In order to present a favorable image, certain points about language and behavior should be remembered.

Activity A: Read this telephone conversation. Decide what is good about it, what is bad about it, and how it can be improved.

Caller: Hello, this is Joseph Smith. I'd like to speak to Mr. Livingstone, please.

Operator: One moment please. I'll connect you.

Secretary: Mr. Livingstone's office.

Caller: May I speak to Mr. Livingstone, please?

Secretary: May I ask in reference to what?

Caller: (getting annoyed) I'm calling about a job.

Secretary: What job is that, sir?

Caller: (getting more annoyed) Stock clerk.

Secretary: Is that the stock clerk at the supply warehouse or the dock warehouse?

Caller: (rudely) The dock warehouse, if it makes that much difference.

Secretary:	One minute, sir. I'll see if Mr. Livingstone is available.
Mr. Livingstone:	This is John Livingstone.
Caller:	I'm calling about a job.
Mr. Livingstone:	In what specific position are you interested?
Caller:	The stock clerk in the dock warehouse.
Mr. Livingstone:	To whom am I speaking?
Caller:	My name is Joseph Smith.
Mr. Livingstone:	What qualifications do you have for this job?
Caller:	I don't know. I never had a job like that before.
Mr. Livingstone:	(sounding bored) Did you graduate from high school?
Caller:	Yeah.
Mr. Livingstone:	(coldly) If you give me your phone number, I'll call you back if we're interested.
Caller:	387-4952.
Mr. Livingstone:	Thank you. We may call you. (hangs up)

Do you think Mr. Livingstone will call Joseph Smith back? Joe did so many things wrong during this phone conversation that he probably lost the chance of getting that job.

The Wrong Way

Let's look over the telephone conversation on pages 84 and 85 and see where Joe went wrong.

First   — Joe lost patience with having to repeat the same information several times.

Second   — Because he was annoyed, Joe did not give all the information he should have given to Mr. Livingstone's secretary. She got a bad impression of him.

Third   — By the time Joe talked to Mr. Livingstone, he'd forgotten all the rules of having a good telephone interview. His answers were not good. He didn't even give his name. Mr. Livingstone had to ask for it.

Fourth   — Joe didn't talk about the personal qualifications he had.

Fifth   — Joe did not answer politely.

Sixth   — Joe did not seem interested in the job.

Seventh   — Joe gave Mr. Livingstone the impression that he really didn't care about the job.

What should Joe have said and done during this telephone conversation? What might have helped Joe to make a good impression during his conversation with the secretary and Mr. Livingstone?

Lesson 4: Analyzing the Mistakes

This is what Joe should have done during his phone conversation.

1. He should have patiently and politely repeated his name and reason for calling to each person to whom he spoke.

2. He should have answered Mr. Livingstone's questions about qualifications by listing *personal qualifications* or characteristics that would help him do a good job. (For example, "I have a good attendance record. I enjoy working with lists and inventories. I keep very accurate records. If I am given directions, I follow them well," and so on.)

3. When applying for a job, he should not have used *slang* (such as "Yeah") or incorrect business English when speaking to anyone.

4. He should use the last name of the person to whom he is speaking, if he can. Calling a person by name is polite and makes a good impression.

5. He should ask what he needed to know about the job. (For example, he could ask about the location of the job, the hours, and the type of work to be done. Some people prefer to discuss salary in person rather than over the phone.)

6. He then should find out if a person wishes him to come in for a job interview; if so, he should ask the time and place.

Joe didn't get to Steps 5 and 6 because Mr. Livingstone cut him off. He had lost interest in talking with Joe. Mr. Livingstone probably decided that Joe was not the kind of person he wanted to hire.

A Better Conversation

Here's what the conversation with Mr. Livingstone might have been like if Joe had handled himself better.

Mr. Livingstone:	This is John Livingstone.
Joe:	Mr. Livingstone, my name is Joseph Smith. I'm calling in answer to your ad in the Sunday *News* for a stock clerk in your dock warehouse.
Mr. Livingstone:	Fine, Mr. Smith. What are your qualifications for the job?
Joe:	Well, sir, I am good at keeping accurate records. I kept records of the stock in a grocery store last summer. I got good grades in math in school. I also had a good attendance record.
Mr. Livingstone:	Did you graduate from high school?
Joe:	Yes, Mr. Livingstone. I graduated in June. Can you tell me something about the job, sir? What would I be doing?
Mr. Livingstone:	Of course. You would be keeping the records of all incoming stock that is received at our dock warehouse. You would also be responsible for letting the foreman know when more stock has to be ordered.
Joe:	I could handle that, sir. Where would I be working?
Mr. Livingstone:	The warehouse on the docks is located at 110 Water Street.
Joe:	Mr. Livingstone, what salary is being offered?
Mr. Livingstone:	The starting pay is $175 per week. If you do well, you would get a $25 a week raise after six months.

Joe:	That salary sounds very good.
Mr. Livingstone:	I am interested in talking with you in person. You sound like someone we'd like to hire. Can you come for an interview tomorrow at 10 a.m.?
Joe:	Yes, sir. Where would I come for the interview?
Mr. Livingstone:	My office is in the Steel Building on the corner of Light and Dark Streets. I'm in Suite 553.
Joe:	(reading his notes) That's the Steel Building, Light and Dark Streets, Suite 553, at 10 o'clock tomorrow morning.
Mr. Livingstone:	That's correct.
Joe:	Thank you, Mr. Livingstone. I'll be there. Good-bye.

Activity A: Number your paper from 1 to 8. If the statement is true, write *True* next to the number. If the statement is not true, write *False* next to the number.

1. Always keep your *tone* of voice polite and patient.
2. Give your name and the reason for calling to the first person who answers the phone. After that, just give your name.
3. If you have no work experience for the job advertised, list the personal qualifications that you think will help you to do a good job.
4. Use the name of the person to whom you are speaking.
5. Never ask how much the pay is.
6. Never use slang or incorrect business English.
7. Take down all the information given and read it back to make sure that it is correct.
8. If the person gives a first name, you may use it when you are speaking.

Lesson 5: Closing the Conversation

Did you notice that in addition to making certain he had the information correct, Joe thanked Mr. Livingstone? He also added that he would be there for the interview. Cynthia and Ruth think that the way you end the conversation is important. People often remember the last thing they heard more than anything else.

Here is another good suggestion about your call. Never continue the conversation too long. The person to whom you are talking has other business to take care of and may grow impatient and annoyed if you continue the conversation too long. Remember that you can give answers to other questions when you are interviewed or when you appear for the job.

Activity A: Number your paper from 1 to 7. Listed below are some statements made during a telephone interview for a job. If you think the statement is a good one, write *Good* next to the number. If you think the statement is bad, write *Bad*. Be prepared to say why each statement is good or bad.

1. "Okay. Yeah, I'll come."
2. "Yes, sir. I'll be there."
3. "Don't talk so fast. I can't get all this stuff down."
4. "Are you paying a good salary?"
5. "What is the pay offered for this job, sir?"
6. "Would you mind going a little slower? I want to make sure that I get all this information down correctly."
7. "Thank you very much. I'll report promptly tomorrow morning at 10:00 a.m. to your office."

Summary

When you must apply by telephone for a job, it is important that you make as good an impression as you can during that conversation.

First   — You must be prepared with the information you need to make the call; for example:
- The exact description or title of the job;
- How you found out about the job;
- Your fact sheet;
- Days and times when you are available for an interview;
- A telephone number where you can be reached.

Second — Speak in a clear, distinct voice. Give your name and your reason for calling.

Third   — Repeat your name and your reason for calling to each person to whom you speak on the telephone.

Fourth — Always be patient and polite.

Fifth   — Answer the questions you are asked as completely as necessary.

Sixth   — Avoid slang. Use good business English.

Seventh — When you know the last name of the person to whom you are talking, use it. Do not use first names.

Eighth   — Ask appropriate questions.

Ninth   — Thank the person with whom you have spoken.

Tenth   — Do not carry on the conversation too long.

CHAPTER REVIEW

Review Activity A: Put these eight activities in the order in which you would do them when applying for a job by telephone. Rewrite the activities in the correct order on a sheet of paper.

- Give my work experience and personal qualifications.
- Know which job was advertised and where I saw it advertised.
- Used a polite and patient tone.
- Have my fact sheet handy.
- Give my name and the reason for my call.
- List the days and times I am available to go for an interview.
- Thank the person for his or her assistance and time.
- Have a pencil and paper handy.

Review Activity B: Write short answers for the six questions listed below.

1. Why is it important for you to speak clearly?
2. Why is it necessary for you to give your name and the reason for your call?
3. Suppose you are asked to give your qualifications and you had no work experience. Why should you say something about your personal qualifications?
4. Why do you want to avoid using slang or incorrect business English?
5. Why should you use the last name of the person to whom you are speaking?
6. Why is it all right to read back the information that you have taken down?

Review Activity C: Below is a list of personal qualifications. If you were applying for the job of stock clerk in the dock warehouse, which of these qualifications would you mention during a telephone interview? On your own paper, write *Yes* or *No* next to the number of each item.

1. I am a member of the Automobile Club.

2. I kept records for the varsity football team.

3. I got good grades in English.

4. I like to go skiing.

5. I was a Scout.

6. I had a good attendance record and was never late.

7. I kept an up-to-date record of all members of the Lions Club.

8. I got good grades in history.

9. I got good grades in math.

10. I enjoy doing paperwork.

11. I enjoy working with my hands and making things.

12. I am a member of the church choir.

13. I live with my mother.

14. I am good at keeping accurate records.

15. I worked in the high school office for a year and got good recommendations from the principal.

16. I do beautiful flower arrangements.

Review Activity D: Number your paper from 1 to 13. Write *True* or *False* for each statement or set of statements.

1. It is important to make a good impression when you call about a job. This call will be the first contact you have with the company.
2. It is not important to be polite to the operator who is connecting you with the person to whom you want to talk.
3. Be prepared before you dial the phone. Have information about the job for which you are applying, how you found out about the job, and so on.
4. You are talking to a person about a job. Saying that you have no qualifications is being honest.
5. Even if you have never done a job like this before, you should mention things that you do well.
6. It is a good idea to have pencil and paper next to you when you make your telephone call.
7. If an employer asks you to come in for an interview, make sure that you can be there on the day and time set.
8. Being able to come in for an interview as soon as possible will probably make a good impression. It will make people think you are eager to get the job.
9. Give a telephone number where you can be reached. Make sure that someone will take a good clear message if the company should call you.
10. Answer politely and patiently.
11. Sounding enthusiastic and eager will probably help you to get the job.
12. If you are more comfortable using slang, use it.
13. Even if you know the last name of the person to whom you are talking, it is not a good idea to use his or her name.

CHAPTER 6

Being Interviewed

Reginald Carter was very nervous. Tomorrow morning he was to go for a *job interview*. His teachers, his parents, and his friends had all warned him. How Reggie acted and looked would have a lot to do with whether or not he would get the job.

Reggie really wanted this job. It was the kind of work he liked. The salary was good. The company was known for looking out for the people who worked there. It would be a good place to work.

It made sense to Reginald to do everything he could to make a good impression. It seemed to him that there were three areas on which he should concentrate. These areas were how businesslike he looked and dressed, how good his answers to the interview questions were, and how well he communicated.

Lesson 1: How You Look

Reggie's mother told him that he should wear a suit or a sports coat and tie. "No matter what job you are applying for, always wear business clothes," she said. She reminded Reggie that everything he planned to wear had to be clean and free of stains.

Reggie had taken his suit to the cleaners so he knew that it was clean. He had a clean shirt and tie. He polished his shoes.

While he was checking his clothes, he looked in the mirror and noticed that he needed a haircut. He went to the barbershop as soon as he finished getting his clothes ready.

That night he trimmed and cleaned his fingernails. The next morning he got up early enough to wash his hair, shower, and shave. He got dressed. Everything he put on was clean and neat. He was careful not to wear much jewelry. He just wore his school ring. Reggie wore appropriate colors. He was not overdressed. Reggie looked just right.

The person who interviews you will base much of his or her opinion of you on how you look. When you walk in, you should look good. "Looking good" for a job interview is not the same as "looking good" for a dance or any other social event.

To look good for a job interview, you must always remember certain suggestions. First, your body and your clothes should be spotless. This suggestion means that you must plan ahead.

If you are going to wear clothes that must be dry cleaned, get them to the cleaners in plenty of time. Make sure that the items that need washing (underwear, shirts, blouses, etc.) are ready at least the day before your interview. Brush or polish your shoes.

Wash your hair and shower. Use deodorant. Brush your teeth carefully. Make certain your fingernails are clean and trimmed. Men will want to shave.

The person who interviews you will be impressed if you and your clothes are clean. Being clean tells people that you care about yourself and others and that people will like being around you.

Activity A: You have a job interview at 9:00 a.m. tomorrow. Draw the chart shown below on a separate sheet of paper. Label the three columns. Write each item listed above the chart in the correct column.

- brush teeth
- get suit cleaned
- wash underwear

- shower
- shave
- wash hair and shirt

- shine shoes
- clean and file nails

Preparing for an Interview		
Two or Three Days Ahead	The Night Before	That Morning

Lesson 2: Be Neat

Being neat at a job interview is as important as being clean. If your hair looks shaggy, you will not impress the interviewer. If your clothes are missing buttons or if your collar is not lying properly, you will seem to be a messy person. To look your neatest, you must plan ahead.

Check the clothes that you plan to wear. Replace any missing buttons or trim. Repair anything that needs mending. Make sure that the repairs you make are neat. Your clothes should be carefully pressed.

If your hair is too long or shaggy, get a haircut. If you have a beard or mustache, trim it. Cut your fingernails if they are different lengths.

When you are dressed and ready to go to the interview, check the way you look. You may check your appearance by using a mirror or by asking someone to check you. Make sure that buttons are fastened correctly and that collars and lapels are folded properly.

Activity A: Add the items listed below to the chart that you drew for the activity in Lesson 1, page 97.

- replace missing buttons
- get a haircut
- trim your fingernails
- make sure collars and lapels are folded properly
- get someone to check you
- check yourself in a mirror
- press your clothes
- repair anything that needs it

Lesson 3: Look Businesslike

The things you pick to wear to an interview should make you look like you are serious about working. A suit is good for a man or a woman. A skirt or pants with a shirt and jacket or sweater is also a good selection.

The colors of the clothes you wear should not be loud. Do not select something that has so much color that it distracts from you. You want people to be tuned in to you, not to what you are wearing.

Limit the amount of jewelry you wear. Many chains or long, dangling earrings are not very businesslike.

Activity A: On a separate sheet of paper, number from 1 to 6. Then complete each of the following sentences. Use the words listed in the box to help you.

long earrings	jewelry	distract
shirt	women	sweater
loud	suit	businesslike
job	pants	jacket

1. When you go to a _____ interview, you should dress in a _____ manner.
2. A _____ is a good choice for both men and _____ .
3. You could also wear a skirt or _____ and a _____ or _____ .
4. The colors of the clothes you wear should not _____ from you.
5. Do not wear _____ colors.
6. Be careful not to wear too much _____ .

Lesson 4: How You Answer Interview Questions

Reginald sat nervously in the waiting room. Finally, the *receptionist* said, "Ms. Short will see you now, Mr. Carter." Reggie made sure that he had thrown away his chewing gum. His teachers had told him that chewing gum made a bad impression on interviewers. He walked in using the best posture he could. He stood straight and tall and introduced himself.

"Hello, Ms. Short. I am Reginald Carter. I'm here to be interviewed."

He waited to sit down until Ms. Short offered him a chair. Then he waited for the first question.

Reggie listened carefully to each question. He thought about his answers and made sure he answered the question that was asked. He replied in a clear, easy-to-understand voice and looked at Ms. Short as he answered. He calmly checked his *fact sheet* or *résumé* if he needed to be sure of a date or an address or the spelling of a name.

When the interview was over, Reginald politely thanked Ms. Short for the interview. He asked when he might hear from her and then left. Reggie had done very well.

Of course, there is no way you can guess what questions you may be asked at an interview. Most of the questions will be asked to find out if you are suited for the job. Answer truthfully and completely. If you don't know the answer to a question, say so. Always be polite.

Activity A: On a separate sheet of paper, list at least five things that Reggie did that might have impressed Ms. Short favorably.

Lesson 5: How You Communicate

The person Ms. Short interviewed after Reggie did not get the job because she communicated so badly. *Communication* is important. There are several ways of letting people know how you feel about something—the kind of language you use, your attitude, and your body language. Body language would include the way you sit or stand and how you look at a person.

Alice Blue, the person who did not get the job, came into Ms. Short's office with her head down and plopped right into a chair. When Ms. Short asked her name, she replied rudely, "What you askin' me that for? Ain't I got an appointment?" She answered Ms. Short's questions by mumbling answers. Ms. Short could not understand some of the things she said.

As Alice answered more questions, she got angry that the interview was taking so long. You could hear the anger in her voice. Soon she got louder. When the interview was over, Alice said, "Yeah, okay," and left.

Alice did not get the job because she used poor grammar and slang. She did not speak clearly and did not answer the questions carefully. Her manners were poor, and she had a nasty attitude.

Reggie got the job because he used good English, spoke clearly, and was polite. He acted like he cared about the interview and answered each question with care.

Reggie understood the importance of communication. He understood that how he communicated was very important during an interview for a job.

Activity A: Listed below are five situations that could come up in a job interview. On a separate sheet of paper, list the letter of the best answer in each case. Explain why your choice is the best answer.

1. The interviewer asks you why you want the job. You say:
    a. "I need the money."
    b. "I'm interested in this kind of work and think that I can do a good job."
    c. "My father told me if I don't get a job, he's going to put me out on the street."

2. The interviewer asks you a question to which you do not know the answer. You say:
    a. "I read about that somewhere. It was in some magazine, I think."
    b. "Whatever you think."
    c. "I'm sorry. I don't know the answer to that question. Perhaps you could tell me what it is."

3. The interviewer tells you this job requires that you work one Saturday a month. You say:
    a. "I can manage that."
    b. "You got to be kiddin'. I don't work on Saturdays."
    c. "I got baseball on Saturdays."

4. The interviewer asks you how your English grades were in school. You say:
    a. "I ain't never got nothin' lower than a C."
    b. "I is the best one in English in my family."
    c. "I got good grades in English."

5. The interviewer asks you why you were fired from your last job. You:
    a. get angry and snap, "I don't know!"
    b. look down at the floor and mumble, "I don't know."
    c. look at the interviewer and say, "I don't know."

Summary

When you go for an interview for a job, you should make sure that you make a good impression. You must look and act your best.

You can make a good impression by wearing the proper clothes and by being and looking clean and neat. In order to look your best, you must plan ahead in order to have things clean and in good repair.

You will want to look businesslike. You will avoid wearing party clothes and items that have loud colors. It is a good idea to avoid too much jewelry, too. Large earrings, rings, or pins are not a good idea. Try to keep what you wear simple.

When you get to the interview, be polite. Introduce yourself and tell why you are there. Answer the interview questions in a clear voice. Listen carefully so you are sure that you are answering the specific questions that you are asked. Look at your fact sheet if you need to check information. Have a copy of your résumé ready to give the person who is interviewing you.

Keep your attitude positive. Be conscious of how you look to the interviewer. Avoid slang and use correct business English.

Following these simple steps will help you to get through a job interview without being too nervous. You will also impress the person interviewing you, and you will have a better chance of getting the job.

CHAPTER REVIEW

Review Activity A: On a sheet of paper, number from 1 to 12. Write the word or words that complete each sentence correctly. Use the words listed in the box to help you. You may use a word as an answer more than once.

cleaners	hair	time	bath	washing
brush	shower	shave	deodorant	clean
nails	teeth	ahead	shine	smile

1. When you go for a job interview, everything about you should be _____ .

2. This statement means that you must plan _____ .

3. If you plan to wear clothing that cannot be washed, allow _____ for you to get them from the _____ .

4. Make sure that things that need _____ are clean.

5. _____ or _____ your shoes.

6. Shampoo your _____ .

7. Take a _____ or a _____ .

8. Be sure to use _____ .

9. Brush your _____ .

10. Clean and trim your _____ .

11. Men will want to _____ .

12. An interviewer knows that you care about yourself and others when you are _____ .

Review Activity B: On a separate piece of paper, number from 1 to 8. If the statement is true, write *True*. If the statement is not true, write *False*.

1. Long, shaggy hair will be fine for an interview if you look good with your hair that way.
2. The interviewer will think that you lost a button just a few minutes ago if a button is missing from your shirt. It will not mean that you may be messy.
3. A collar that is not folded correctly may make you look messy.
4. If a seam is coming apart, fix it before you go to your interview.
5. When you mend something that you plan to wear to an interview, fix it neatly.
6. If you have a beard or a mustache, trim it.
7. Broken nails look okay.
8. Don't bother other people to find out how you look.

Review Activity C: Given below is a list of clothes, jewelry, and shoes. On a separate sheet of paper, make two columns. Write items from the list that are appropriate to wear for a job interview in column one. Write items that are inappropriate for a job interview in column two.

jeans	gold high heels	jogging suit
gold hoop earrings	a school ring	tennis shoes
loafers	low-heeled pumps	shorts
a pleated blue skirt	six gold chains	a bra-type top
sandals	large bangle bracelet	cutoffs
a suit	a sports jacket	a sweater
a shirt and tie	undershirt as outerwear	a sweat shirt

Review Activity D: On a separate sheet of paper, rewrite the information below. The new paragraph should tell the **best** way to handle an interview.

Bill slumped into the room and plopped down. He said, "Okay, what's the scoop?" When the interviewer asked a question, Bill didn't know the answer so he made something up. He forgot to bring his fact sheet so he made up a date and an address. When he was told that the interview was over, he didn't say anything. He just got up and left.

Review Activity E: On a separate sheet of paper, rewrite the five sentences below. Correct the errors in each sentence.

1. Ain't I got an appointment?
2. My name be Estelle.
3. I doesn't know that.
4. Yeah, okay.
5. I think that you and me will get along fine.

CHAPTER 7

Beginning Your Job

Paul and Ernest both reported to work at the same time for their first day at Karl's Appliance Company. They had never met one another. They just happened to be told to report for their first day at the same time.

By the end of the first week, Paul no longer had a job. Ernest was doing just fine. What happened to them could happen to you. Let's take a look at their first day.

The first thing that Paul and Ernest were asked to do was to fill out a *W-4 form*. This form is put out by the Internal Revenue Service. The IRS is part of the Department of Treasury of the United States government. The law says that you must complete this form when you are hired so that your employer can hold back from each pay a part of the taxes that you will probably owe the government at the end of the year. Paul didn't know the first thing about the form. Ernest had done quite a bit of reading and knew something about the W-4.

Paul used up three forms and didn't get one done right. Ernest filled his out correctly the first time. Ernest read the instructions carefully and understood them. Paul tried to read the instructions, but he didn't understand them. On the fourth try, Paul still made a mistake so that more money would have been taken out of his pay than was necessary.

Reading tax forms of any kind can be confusing. You need practice to understand what you are doing and to fill out the forms correctly.

Lesson 1: The Vocabulary on Form W-4

Before you can begin to understand the W-4 form, you need to know the words that are used on the form and its directions.

Withholding: An amount of money that the business you work for subtracts from your salary. This part of your salary is not paid to you. It is paid directly to the Internal Revenue Service as part or all of your income tax.

Allowances: Things the government will consider when deciding what amount of money will be withheld from salary as income tax.

Personal allowances: You can claim from none to several allowances. You can claim a personal allowance for yourself. If you are married, you can claim an allowance for your husband or wife (your spouse). You can claim additional allowances if your spouse does not work. Other personal allowances (for example, for dependents) are also described on a W-4 form. The more personal allowances you claim, the less money will be withheld from your pay as taxes. Claiming fewer allowances means that more money will be withheld. However, you must honestly claim only the allowances to which you are entitled.

Dependents: Children or other people who may not work and who count on you for over half of their needs (food, shelter, clothing, etc.).

Your spouse: Your husband or wife.

Exemption: A release from the requirement of taxation; some reason why money does not have to be withheld as taxes from your pay.

Deductions: Expenses considered when determining taxable income; you do not pay taxes on some expenses (donations to charities, home mortgage interest payments, state and local taxes, etc.).

Maximum: The most; the largest amount.

Minimum: The least; the smallest amount.

Activity A: Number your paper from 1 to 9. Match the income tax term in the first column with its meaning or explanation in the second column. Write the correct letter next to each number.

Term	Meaning
1. your spouse	a. The largest amount
2. minimum	b. You can claim one for yourself
3. allowances	c. Expenses the government considers in deciding what amount of money will be withheld from your wages
4. dependents	
5. deductions	
6. withholding	d. Expenses you pay for which you do not have to pay taxes
7. maximum	
8. personal allowances	e. Your husband or wife
9. exemption	f. The part of your salary that is paid to the IRS as income tax
	g. The least
	h. People who count on you for food, clothing, and shelter
	i. A reason why you do not have to have money withheld from your wages

Form **W-4**	**Employee's Withholding Allowance Certificate**	OMB No. 1545-0010
Department of the Treasury Internal Revenue Service	▶ For Privacy Act and Paperwork Reduction Act Notice, see reverse.	19**93**

1	Type or print your first name and middle initial	Last name		2	Your social security number

Home address (number and street or rural route)	3 ☐ Single ☐ Married ☐ Married, but withhold at higher Single rate.
	Note: If married, but legally separated, or spouse is a nonresident alien, check the Single box.
City or town, state, and ZIP code	4 If your last name differs from that on your social security card, check
	here and call 1-800-772-1213 for more information · · · · ▶ ☐

5	Total number of allowances you are claiming (from line G above or from the worksheets on page 2 if they apply) .	5	
6	Additional amount, if any, you want withheld from each paycheck	6	$
7	I claim exemption from withholding for 1993 and I certify that I meet **ALL** of the following conditions for exemption:		

• Last year I had a right to a refund of **ALL** Federal income tax withheld because I had **NO** tax liability; **AND**
• This year I expect a refund of **ALL** Federal income tax withheld because I expect to have **NO** tax liability; **AND**
• This year if my income exceeds $600 and includes nonwage income, another person cannot claim me as a dependent.

If you meet all of the above conditions, enter "EXEMPT" here . . . . ▶ | 7 |

Under penalties of perjury, I certify that I am entitled to the number of withholding allowances claimed on this certificate or entitled to claim exempt status.

Employee's signature ▶	Date ▶	, 19
8 Employer's name and address (Employer: Complete 8 and 10 only if sending to the IRS)	9 Office code (optional)	10 Employer identification number

Cat. No. 10220Q

Activity B: Study the W-4 form shown at the top of this page. On a separate sheet of paper, write the information you would fill out for items 1, 2, and 3.

1. Type or print your full name.
   Home address (number and street or rural route)
   City or town, state, and ZIP code
2. Your Social Security number
3. Marital status ☐ Single
   ☐ Married
   ☐ Married, but withhold at higher Single rate

Lesson 2: More About the W-4 Form

Now we get to the part that gave Paul the most difficulty. He read the instructions but had trouble understanding them. Ernest didn't have as much trouble. Let's see if you can do as well as Ernest did. On the next page is a set of some directions for the W-4 form. Read them carefully.

A. Enter "1" for **yourself** if no one else can claim you as a
   dependent ....A _____

B. Enter "1" if
   1. You are single and have only one job; or
   2. You are married, have only one job, and
      your spouse does not work; or
   3. Your wages from a second job or your ....B _____
      spouse's wages (or the total of both) are
      $2500 or less

C. Enter "1" for your **spouse**. But you may choose to enter "0"
   if you are married and have either a working spouse or
   more than one job (This may help you avoid having
   too little tax withhheld) ....C _____

Activity A: Number from 1 to 5 on your paper. Answer these questions.

1. On line A, can you claim yourself if your father claims you as a
   dependent? When can you claim yourself?
2. If you and your wife both work, what can you enter on line C?
3. You are single and earned $1,987 on a second job. What do you enter
   on line B?
4. You have one job; you spouse doesn't work. Where may you enter
   "1"?
5. You have one job and are not married. Where do you enter "1"?

Your salary, the people who are your dependents ,and your expenses
will determine how you complete the W-4 form. Tax rules also change
from one year to the next. You may need to have more or less money
withheld from your pay. If you do not understand how to complete this
form, ask your employer or someone in the accounting department of
your company. You may also call the Internal Revenue Service. Because
tax rules change, it is important to know the rules for the current year.

Lesson 3: Company Rules and Regulations

Once Paul and Ernest had finished filling out their W-4 forms, they were given a list of company regulations. They were told to read the list carefully. These rules were meant for all employees. If employees broke the rules, they could be fired. Take a look at this company's rules.

Karl's Appliance Company
Employees' Regulations

1. **Working Hours**

   Working hours are 8:30 a.m. to 5:00 p.m. You are allowed one 15-minute coffee break daily. Your lunch period runs from 12 noon to 12:30 p.m.

   All employees are required to punch the time clock at the start and finish of each day and also before and after the lunch break. You are responsible for your own *time card*. It is forbidden for you to punch another person's time card. You will be paid according to the record shown by your time card.

2. **Employee Status**

   All new employees will be considered on *probation* for the first six months they are employed. Any employee may be placed on probation if his or her work is less than satisfactory for any given evaluation period.

3. **Wage Policies**

   After six months of satisfactory service, you will receive a raise in pay and be removed from probation status. Other pay raises will be given annually.

   You will be paid each Friday for the work done the week before.

Activity A: Number from 1 to 10 on a sheet of paper. Then read the following statements. If the statement is true, write *True* next to the number of the statement. If the statement is not true, write *False* next to the number.

1. At Karl's Appliance Company, employees can eat whenever they want as long as they don't take over 30 minutes.
2. You must be at work by 8:30 in the morning and you may leave at 5:00 in the evening.
3. You get one 15-minute coffee break.
4. You must punch the time clock four times each day.
5. You can punch other peoples' time cards for them if they are in a hurry.
6. Your pay will depend upon what time your foreman says you worked.
7. For the first six months that you work at Karl's, you will be on probation.
8. If your work isn't good, you can be placed on probation.
9. When you get off probation after working for the company for six months, you will get a raise.
10. You will get a pay raise once every six months.

Activity B: If you begin work on Monday, March 5, when will you get your first pay?

Hint: Remember, according to the company rules and regulations, you will be paid each Friday for the work that you did the week before.

More Regulations

Paul and Ernest continued reading the company rules. There seemed to be rules about everything. Paul got angry. "You can't do anything around here. Boy, they really watch you. It's like a prison," Paul remarked to Ernest.

"Oh, I think the rules make sense. They have a business to run. You can't expect to be able to do just what you want to," replied Ernest. "Look at these rules. They seem fair."

General Policies

1. You are expected to be at your work station by 8:30 a.m. If you are sick, you must call your *foreman* by 8:30 a.m. Absence and lateness on a consistent basis will be grounds for dismissal.

2. Smoking is restricted to certain areas of the building for reasons of health and safety. Obey the posted signs.

3. The switchboard will call you to the phone only in case of emergency. Other calls may not be received during working hours.

4. If your foreman rates your work unsatisfactory, you will be given six months in which to bring up your rating. If you have not done so by that time, you will be dismissed.

"I hate these rules," Paul grumbled. "I hate getting up in the morning, and I never get anywhere on time. If I don't feel like comin' in, I ain't. And I'd like to see them say I can't smoke somewhere."

Ernest didn't say a word. He gave Paul a funny look and went on reading.

Activity C: Number from 1 to 8 on a separate sheet of paper. Then answer the following questions.

1. It takes you half an hour to get to work. You are due at your *workstation* at 8:30 a.m. You can get a bus that leaves your corner at 7:40 a.m., another that leaves your corner at 7:50 a.m., and another that leaves your corner at 8:00 a.m. Which bus or buses could you take to go to work? Why?

2. If you are going to be out sick, what should you do at Karl's Appliance Company?

3. Why is smoking restricted to some areas of the building? How will you know where you can smoke and where you can't smoke?

4. If you get an emergency call during working hours, what will happen?

5. Why might it be a good idea to tell your family and friends not to call you at work unless there is a real emergency?

6. In June your foreman rates your work as unsatisfactory. By what month must you bring up that rating? What will happen if you don't get a satisfactory rating?

7. Is Paul's attitude good or bad? Why?

8. Is Ernest's attitude good or bad? Why?

Lesson 4: Getting to Your Workstation

After Paul and Ernest had read the company rules, they were sent to their workstations. Karl's Appliance Company is in a big building, so they were given a floor plan or a map to help them find their way. Paul was to report to workstation B. Ernest was to report to workstation D.

Here is a copy of the map that was given to Paul and Ernest:

Karl's Appliance Company
Floor Plan

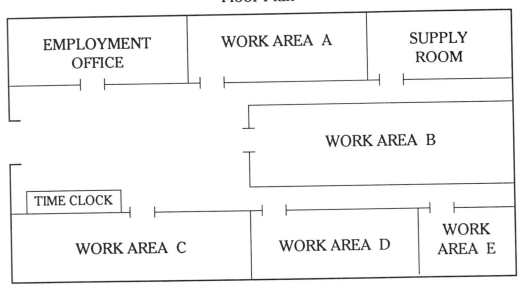

Paul didn't even try to read the floor plan. He didn't think that was important. He walked out of the employment office and headed right for the supply room. Some men laughed at him when he walked into the wrong room. The laughter made him angry and embarrassed.

Ernest read the floor plan for Karl's Appliance Company. He walked straight to work area D. He didn't have to worry about being embarrassed at losing his way.

Activity A: Study the floor plan of Karl's Appliance Company. Then answer the following questions on a separate sheet of paper.

 1. Why do you think the time clock is placed near the front door?
 2. If you had to go from work area C to work area E, in what direction would you turn when you walked out of the door of work area C?
 3. Which work area is farthest away from the employment office?
 4. Once they have punched the time clock, which workers will get to their work area first?
 5. Which work area is the largest?
 6. Which work area is the smallest?
 7. How many supply rooms are there?
 8. Which work area does not share a wall with any office or work area?
 9. Why do you think the employment office is near the front door?
10. How many work areas are shown on this floor plan?

Activity B: Use a separate sheet of paper. Draw a floor plan of the first floor of your house, or of the apartment or room, in which you live. Then write a set of five questions about that floor plan. Working with a classmate, trade floor plans and questions. Look at your classmate's floor plan and answer the five questions. See how good you are at drawing a floor plan and how good you are at reading one.

Lesson 5: On the Job

As soon as Paul and Ernest got to their work areas, each of them was given safety rules for that area. Their foremen told them to read the safety rules before they did anything else. Here are the rules they were given.

Karl's Appliance Company
Safety Regulations

1. Do **not** operate any machine for which you have not been trained unless you are being supervised by an officially appointed employee.

2. Be sure all safety devices are in place before operating any machine.

3. In case of a breakdown or faulty operation, shut off all machinery and report to your foreman.

4. Long hair, open-toed shoes, neckties, rings, loose clothing, and jewelry of any kind are forbidden in the work areas. *Lockers* are supplied in which to keep your clothes and valuables.

Paul glanced at the rules and began to walk around his work area. Paul pushed a switch. He didn't know what it was for, but he soon found out. Suddenly he heard this funny noise. His foreman shouted, "Turn off that machine. It's jamming. What the heck is wrong here?"

When the foreman found out that Paul had pushed the switch, he got very angry. "Look, jerk," he shouted at Paul, "The safety rules say that you aren't to touch anything until someone is there to show you how to work the machine and watch you work it! Can't you read, stupid?"

Paul was in trouble again.

Ernest read the rules. Then told the foreman he was ready to learn how to use the machine. The foreman got someone to teach Ernest how to use the machine to which he was assigned.

Activity A: Listed below are some safety rules for Karl's Appliance Company. However, a part of each rule has been left out. On a separate sheet of paper, complete each rule.

1. You are not to try to work any machine unless _____ .
2. All _____ before you operate any machine.
3. In case the machine breaks, _____ and _____ .
4. If the machine is not working right, _____ and _____ .
5. The following things are forbidden in the work areas: _____ , _____ , _____ , _____ , _____ , and _____ .
6. _____ are supplied as a safe place in which employees can keep clothing and valuables.

The Outcome

All week long Paul did just what he felt like doing. He got to work late. One day he didn't come in, and he didn't bother to call. He kept fooling with machines that he was supposed to leave alone. He caused one machine to break down. It couldn't be used until it was fixed. It took two days to get it repaired. That delay cost the company a large amount of money.

All week long Ernest did just what he was told to do. He paid attention and learned fast. He followed all the rules, got to work a few minutes early every day, and was not absent. He was polite and kind to the people around him. Oh, he made a few mistakes. After all, he was just learning. His foreman didn't get angry. He knew that Ernest was trying to do a good job.

At the end of the week, Paul got fired. Ernest got a pat on the back.

Evaluation

Nearly all companies judge the performance of their employees on a regular basis. The *evaluation* is usually done by the *immediate supervisor.* How well an employee does on an evaluation can determine whether the employee keeps the job, is promoted, and gets a raise in pay.

If you are anything like Ernest, you will want to do well on each evaluation. It is helpful to know the areas in which you are evaluated. While evaluations vary from one business to another, most do have some common areas that the supervisor considers when judging your performance. These six questions are often included on evaluations.

1. *How well do you know your job?*
   If you do not need to be told over and over again what to do, you might be rated high in this item.

2. *What is the quality of your work?*
   If you make few mistakes and you finish each job, you will probably rate high in this area.

3. *How much work do you produce?*
   If you work at a good pace and stay on schedule, you may score high on this item.

4. *How dependable are you?*
   If you follow directions and regulations, you may score well on this item.

5. *What kind of attitude do you have?*
   If you are cooperative and careful, if you take pride in the job you do, and if you get along with your fellow workers, you may score high on this item.

6. *What is your attendance like?*
   If you come to work regularly and are not late, you will probably score well on this item.

When you begin a new job, you should remember these points and work toward being the best worker you can.

You can become a good employee by learning to do your job well, working accurately, turning out the amount of work expected of you, being dependable, having a positive attitude, and coming to work regularly and on time.

If you score high in all six of these areas, you should do well when you are evaluated by your immediate supervisor.

Activity B: Listed below are nine descriptions of workers. Read them carefully. Look back at the six areas described on pages 120 and 121. Write the area in which each employee seems to be weakest.

1. Mary has worked for the company for six months. She never seems to know what she should be doing. She always waits until her supervisor tells her what to do next.

2. Jim works at a job where he is expected to turn out a certain amount of material each day. Jim stops a lot. He looks out the window, and he reads his newspaper.

3. Maude is careless. The work she does often needs to be redone, repaired, or thrown out.

4. Sheldon comes to work regularly, but he is always late. He has been late fourteen times in the last thirty days. He always has some excuse, such as that the bus was late or his alarm clock didn't go off.

5. Selma really gets annoyed when her supervisor points out something she is doing wrong. She sulks and pouts and takes her anger out on the people with whom she works.

6. Betty does what she wants to do when she wants to do it. She can be a good worker when she feels like it, but she often ignores company rules.

7. Don is well liked by his supervisor and his fellow employees. However, he doesn't always pay attention to directions. He makes a lot of mistakes.

8. Fran misses a lot of time from work. She always seems to have something wrong with her.

9. George does a good enough job most of the time. However, he works for a company where employees must work odd shifts and must work overtime at some busy times. George never offers to work an odd shift and never offers to work overtime.

Summary

Since you want to do well on your job, like Ernest, let's review briefly your first few days on the job. One of the first things you will have to do is fill out a W-4 form. You must complete this form so that your employer can hold back from each pay an amount of money that will go to the Internal Revenue Service as payment of all or part of your income tax. It is important that this form be filled out correctly so that the proper amount of money can be withheld. If too little money is withheld, you may have a large tax bill at the end of the year. If too much money is withheld, you may not take enough wages home to pay all your bills.

You will also need to read and understand the rules and regulations of the company for which you work. If you do not understand them, ask your supervisor to explain them. If you fail to follow these rules, you may end up losing your job. Companies also have safety rules to keep the employees from getting hurt, to keep the machinery from getting broken, and to follow the rules of their own insurance policies. You should respect these safety rules and live by them.

If you work for a large company, it is important to be able to find your way around. Some companies provide new employees with floor plans. Others use signs posted around the building. Still others have no special method. It is up to you to be wise enough to ask questions and to learn your way around the building where you work.

The first few days on a job can be confusing and frustrating. It takes time to adjust and to learn the ropes. If you take your time, ask questions, and follow the rules and regulations, you should do well. Because most companies have some way to judge workers, doing well will help you to get promotions and raises.

CHAPTER REVIEW

Review Activity A: On a separate sheet of paper, number from 1 to 8. Then choose the word or words from the box that best completes each sentence. Write the correct word or words next to each number. You will use each answer only once.

job	W-4 form	spouse
personal allowance	minimum	maximum
Internal Revenue Service	earn	withhold

1. The _____ is filled out by everyone who works.
2. This form is used to decide how much your employer will _____ from your paycheck.
3. This money subtracted from your pay is paid to the _____ for part or all of your income tax.
4. On that form you may take a _____ for yourself.
5. If your _____ does not work, you may take an additional allowance.
6. You may also have to consider a second _____ .
7. How much you _____ on that job will determine if you can claim an additional allowance.
8. You will probably want to have the _____ amount taken out of your wages so that you will have to pay only a _____ amount of extra taxes at the end of the year.

Review Activity B: On your own paper, write the answers to these questions about yourself.

1. How many allowances can you claim?
2. Do you have any dependents? Who are they?
3. What other deductions could you claim that might affect the amount of tax you have to pay?
4. Do you have a spouse? Does your spouse work?
5. Did you get a large *refund* from your taxes last year? Should you decrease the amount withheld from your wages because of this refund?
6. Did you have to pay a large amount of additional taxes last year? How can you keep from doing that this year?

Review Activity C: Read the rule below. Then look at the statements below this rule. Number your paper from 1 to 5. Write *True* next to the number if the statement is true. Write *False* if the statement is not true.

> The use or sale of alcohol, marijuana, or any drugs on these premises is forbidden by law. Any employee breaking this rule will be dismissed immediately and have criminal charges placed against him or her.

1. It is okay to use alcohol and drugs as long as you don't sell them.
2. You could be arrested if you are caught using drugs.
3. You can sell marijuana but not use it on the premises.
4. You are not only breaking a company rule when you use drugs on the premises, you are also breaking the law.
5. If you use drugs on company property, you will either be fired or charged with a crime but not both.

Review Activity D: Read the company regulation given below. Then, on a separate sheet of paper, answer the following questions about that regulation.

Regulation 6:
   If you have a grievance with your foreman, submit your complaint in writing and state the reasons for your grievance. A meeting will be held with you, your foreman, and his supervisor to discuss your grievance. The supervisor will determine what further action, if any, will be taken.

---

1. What is a grievance?
2. If you have a grievance with your foreman, what should you do?
3. What will happen after you put your grievance in writing?
4. Who makes the final decision about your grievance?
5. What does this regulation say to do if you have a grievance against a fellow worker?

Review Activity E: Listed below are six questions that most companies use to evaluate employees. However, the words in the questions are scrambled. Unscramble each sentence. Write the complete sentences on your own paper.

1. attitude have kind do you of what
2. of work what the is your quality
3. you job know how well your do
4. like is attendance your what
5. work much you how produce do
6. are how dependable you

Review Activity F: Given below is a floor plan of the second floor of an office building. Study this floor plan. Then answer the following questions on a separate piece of paper.

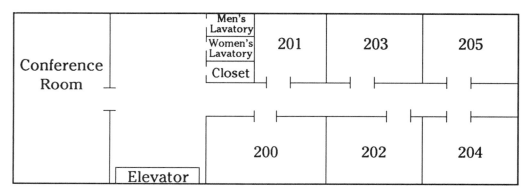

1. As you get off the elevator, which way would you turn to get to Room 205?

2. As you get off the elevator, which way would you turn to get to the conference room?

3. Which is closer to the elevator—the men's lavatory or the women's?

4. What separates Room 204 from Room 205?

5. What kind of numbering is used for the offices that are to the right as you get off the elevator?

6. What room is across the hall from Room 202?

7. Suppose that you are in Room 205 and you want to get a broom from the closet. In what direction would you go—right or left?

8. What office is nearest to the conference room?

9. When people leave Room 200 to go to the elevator, in which direction do they turn?

Review Activity G: Number your paper from 1 to 12.   Read each statement. If it is true, write *True* next to the number. If it is not true, write *False*.

1. Nearly all companies have some kind of employee evaluation.

2. These evaluations are usually done by the president of the company.

3. If you need to be told over and over again how to do your job, you will probably be rated well for asking questions.

4. In order for you to be rated well on the quality of your work, you must be accurate and thorough.

5. If you don't produce as much work as your company thinks you should, you can get a low evaluation in that area.

6. Employees are never evaluated on whether or not they follow company rules and regulations.

7. Your attitude can affect your evaluation.

8. Attendance is important when you are evaluated, but whether or not you are often late doesn't matter.

9. The way you get along with the other employees may affect your evaluation.

10. Knowing your job is an important part of getting a good evaluation.

11. The immediate supervisor is often the person who does the evaluation.

12. It is helpful to keep in mind the traits on which you will be evaluated.

CHAPTER 8

Learning How to Get Along

The first week on her first job was wonderful for Sue because her foreman had assigned her a "buddy." Sue's buddy was Phil Anton. He helped her through a number of new situations. After Sue had gone through all of the paperwork she had to do before starting her job, Phil trained her to use the sorting machine. She did pretty well that first day.

When she got to work on the second day, she realized that no one had shown her how to fill in her *time card*. She got a blank card from the box near the clock. Then she read it carefully. She thought she could figure out what to do. Just then Phil Anton, smiling, came through the front door. "Oh, Phil," said Sue, "I'm glad you got here. I want to make sure I fill out my time card correctly."

As Sue filled out her time card, Phil watched and helped her to learn what to do.

Lesson 1: Reading Time Cards

The time card had a heading that looked like this:

Date _____
              From   To

WEEKLY TIME CARD

(Notice: This card must be turned in to the proper authority before payment can be made.)

Name _____
Address _____
Position _____   Dept. _____
Soc. Sec. No. _____   Badge No. _____

It seemed pretty simple. Still, Sue wasn't sure what to put in the blank marked "Date." Phil explained that at their company the *pay week* started on Tuesday. Since today was Tuesday, the first date Sue should put in was today's date. That would take care of the "From" part of the blank. Then she was to put in the coming Monday's date. That would take care of the "To" part of the blank. Phil explained that Sue used Monday's date because on each Tuesday she would fill out a new time card. Each time card went from Tuesday to the following Monday.

Sue also wanted to know what was meant by *"Position."* Phil explained that that line was for the name of the job Sue was doing. "Oh, that's easy!" exclaimed Sue. "I'm a sorting machine operator."

"Right," said Phil. "Any other questions?"

"No, I'm fine now," smiled Sue. "Thanks to you."

Activity A: Given below is the top part of another time card. It is slightly different from Sue's, but you should have no trouble understanding it. Notice that each blank is numbered. Below the time card are lists of items that three different employees would use to fill in those blanks. On a separate sheet of paper, number from 1 to 6 three times. Then, next to each number, write the letter of the item that each employee would put on that line.

The Hall Distribution Company

EMPLOYEE TIME CARD

Date _____(1)_____   (2)_____

            From   To

Employee's Full Name _____(3)_____

Position ____(4)_____   Foreman ____(5)_____

Signature _____(6)_____

---

1. a. Bill Chang
    b. 1/13/94
    c. Susan R. Jones

    d. *Susan R. Jones*
    e. 1/7/94
    f. Sorter

2. a. *Claude B. Rivers*
    b. 1/20/94
    c. Packer

    d. 1/14/94
    e. Claude B. Rivers
    f. Shirley Combs

3. a. Shipping Clerk
    b. 1/26/94
    c. 1/20/94

    d. Roger Martin
    e. *Roger Martin*
    f. Phillip Fine

Lesson 2: Reading Work Schedules

As they walked to their work area, Phil told Sue that each week on Monday she had better make sure to check the *work schedule.* "This is not a 9 to 5 place," Phil said. "Our hours vary depending upon the work load. Some weeks you may come in early and leave early or come late and leave late because we have an extra shift working."

On Monday Sue went to the bulletin board in her work area and checked the work schedule. Phil had been right. Starting the next day, she was due in to work at 6 a.m. and would be leaving at 2:30 p.m.

On Tuesday, when Sue reported to work a few minutes before 6, her foreman was pleased. He told her that some new people forgot about checking the work schedule. They lost pay because they did not get to work when they were due. Sue was glad that hadn't happened to her.

When she had a chance to talk to Phil during their lunch break, she thanked him for his reminder. She said, "You are a great help. I would have lost pay if you hadn't reminded me to check the work schedule on Monday."

If Sue had reported to work at 8 a.m. instead of 6, she would have lost two hours of pay. Sue's pay comes to $5.95 an hour. How much would it have cost her if she had reported late? If you figured $11.90, you were right.

What do you think Sue's foreman would have thought of her if she had been late? He certainly wouldn't have gotten a good impression of her. It might seem as if she had bad habits and was not going to be a good employee.

Below is the schedule that Sue had to check. See if you can understand it.

```
┌─────────────────────────────────────────────────┐
│  WORK SCHEDULE — WEEK OF 1/14                     │
│                               Shift               │
│  Anton, Phil ....................8:30  a.m.        │
│  Carling, Ed ...................6:00  a.m.         │
│  Edwards, Jean .............3:30  p.m.             │
│  Gerald, Mary.................8:30  a.m.           │
│  Jones, Susan ................6:00  a.m.           │
│  Moore, Simon .............8:30  a.m.              │
│  Ratz, Bob.......................6:00  a.m.        │
│  Williams, Nancy ..........3:30  p.m.             │
└─────────────────────────────────────────────────┘
```

Notice that the line at the top tells what week this schedule is for. At the left are listed the names of the employees. In the right-hand column are the times they are to report to work. There seem to be three *shifts*, or scheduled work periods. Can you figure out what they are?

Activity A: Answer these questions. Use a separate sheet of paper.

1. What are the times to report for each of the three shifts?
2. Do Sue and Phil work on the same shift this week?
3. Who does work on the same shift with Phil?
4. Who works on the same shift with Sue?
5. Who works on the 3:30 p.m. shift?
6. For what week is this schedule?
7. How many workers does this schedule include?
8. At what time does Simon Moore report to work?
9. At what time does Bob Ratz report?

Activity B: Figure out the time when each of the three shifts ends. Each employee works an $8^1/_2$-hour shift.

Lesson 3: Following Directions

So far Sue had done very well following directions. When she wasn't sure about something, she asked someone she could trust. Sue knew that being able to follow directions well is an important part of every job. She knew that to keep her job she must make as few mistakes as possible. Making few mistakes means reading directions carefully.

Sue's job requires the lifting and moving of heavy boxes. Here are the directions she has been given by the company for doing this part of her job. Sue's *insurance coverage* may not pay benefits if she is injured as a result of not following such safety procedures.

Lifting and Moving Boxes

1. Check the area in which you will be moving the boxes.

2. Clear the floor of all objects that may cause you to trip.

3. Make sure the boxes will fit through doorways.

4. To lift, squat close to the box with one foot beside it and one foot behind it. Grasp the box in both palms and fingers. Keep both arms close to the body. Lift the box by straightening both legs.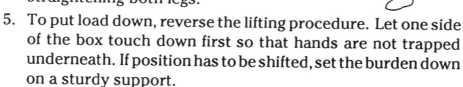

5. To put load down, reverse the lifting procedure. Let one side of the box touch down first so that hands are not trapped underneath. If position has to be shifted, set the burden down on a sturdy support.

WARNING: Employee's insurance coverage will not be effective if proper lifting procedures are not followed.

Activity A: Listed below are the directions that Sue was given for lifting boxes. They have been reworded, and they are out of order. On a separate piece of paper, number from 1 to 5. Put the directions in the correct order. Write the letter next to the number that indicates the order in which each direction should be listed.

a.   Check to see if the doorways are wide enough for the boxes.

b.   When putting the box down, let one side of the box touch first so that you can get your hands out.

c.   Check the area in which you will be moving with the box.

d.   Squat close to the box. Put one foot beside the box. Put the other foot behind it. Hold the box in both hands close to your body. Lift the box by straightening both legs.

e.   Clear the floor and the surrounding area of anything that is in your way.

Activity B: You probably noticed the warning at the bottom of the directions for lifting boxes. This warning said: "Employee's insurance coverage will not be effective if proper lifting procedures are not followed."

1.   Rewrite that statement in your own words. Make sure that you keep the real meaning of the statement.

2.   Write the answers to these questions.

   a.   What could happen to Sue if she did not follow these directions for lifting and moving boxes?

   b.   Why would she lose her insurance coverage if she does not follow the lifting procedures?

Written Directions

After Phil taught Sue to use the sorting machine, her foreman gave her a list of directions. "Sue," he said, "These are directions for keeping your machine in the best possible running condition. Read them and make sure you follow them. If you have any questions, see me."

Sue read the directions carefully. Then she carefully made herself a *schedule.* Look at the list of directions. Why did Sue make a schedule?

The Care of the Sorting Machine

1. Always turn machine off when you leave the work area.
2. Oil the starter mechanism once each week.
3. Oil the rotary wheels once a day.
4. Oil the tray lifts once a month.
5. Dust it daily with an oiled cloth before using.
6. Do not try to repair the machine yourself. If something goes wrong, notify the foreman immediately.

Do you see why Sue made a schedule? Right! There were some things she had to do every day, some things once a week, and some things once a month. Here's her schedule. Did she leave anything off her schedule? Is it accurate?

First (every day) — Dust with oiled cloth.
Second (every day) — Oil rotary wheels.
Monday — Oil starter.
First Monday of the month — Oil tray lifts.

Reminder 1: Turn OFF machine when you leave work area.
Reminder 2: If anything goes wrong, call foreman.

Sue tacked her schedule onto her work table and checked it off to make certain she had done everything she was supposed to do. If you said that Sue did not leave anything out and that her schedule was accurate, you are correct. She did a good job of reading and understanding the directions. Now let's see if you can do as well.

Activity C: Listed below is a set of directions. Read the directions carefully. Then answer the following questions. Write the answers on a separate sheet of paper.

Unjamming a Dispenser

1. Turn off the switch.
2. Place a 1 x 2-inch board so it rests against one of the empellers.
3. Using the wood piece as a lever, work the turntable back and forth. Repeat this motion until the jam is dislodged.
4. Push the RESET button to restart the motor.

---

1. What tools do you need to unjam a disposer?
2. How do you use the piece of wood?
3. How big should the piece of wood be?
4. What do you do with the turntable? How long do you do this?
5. Why is Step #1 in the directions important?
6. Why is Step #4 in the directions important?
7. In what order are these directions listed?

Activity D: Read these directions for changing a typewriter ribbon. Then write *True* or *False* for each of the following statements.

Changing a Typewriter Ribbon

1. Be sure the ribbon load lever is in the load position.
2. Put the uninked part of the ribbon over the outside of the guidepost and the ribbon guides. Failure to do so will cause ribbon breakage.
3. Position the ribbon cartridge so that it fits between the spring clips. Firmly push down both ends of the cartridge.
4. Thread the uninked portion through the ribbon guides.
5. Turn the knob on the cartridge in the direction of the arrow until the uninked portion disappears inside the cartridge.
6. Move ribbon load lever to the type position.
7. Close cover.

---

1. Be sure the ribbon load lever is in the type position before you put in the new cartridge.
2. If you do not put the uninked part of the ribbon over the outside of the guidepost, the ribbon will break.
3. After you have made sure the ribbon load lever is in the load position, you should put the uninked part of the ribbon over the outside of the guidepost and the ribbon guides.
4. During Step 3, you position the ribbon guides so that they fit between the spring clips.
5. Once the ribbon cartridge fits between the spring clips, you press firmly down on both ends of the cartridge.
6. The next step is to thread the uninked part of the ribbon through the ribbon guides.
7. Turn the knob on the cartridge in opposite direction of the arrow.

8. When the uninked part of the cartridge disappears, you should move the ribbon load lever to the load position.
9. Close the cover of the typewriter before typing.

Lesson 4: Helping Your Memory

Sue found that on her first week on the new job many people were giving her directions. Most of these directions were told to her and not written down. After the first day, Sue realized that she was having trouble remembering everything people said. It was just too much to remember all at one time. She got a small memo book. She kept this book, along with a pencil, in the pocket of her coveralls. When someone told her something, she took down notes. She didn't write every word people said. She just wrote down important or *key words* to help her remember what they said. She found that this practice helped her and saved her from asking questions more than once.

On her second day, Phil told her, "When you start the sorter, set the dial on 5. Once it is working smoothly, move it slowly up to 7. Never put the dial past 7 unless the foreman tells you to."

This is what Sue wrote in her memo book. "Set 5, when working smoothly, move slowly to 7. Never past 7." Sue got all the important ideas. She left out those things she would remember once she saw what she had written. For example, she knew that when she saw "set 5," she would know that that direction meant when she started the sorter.

Later that day, her foreman told her, "The paper loader should never get below a thousand. Refill the loader at about 1500." Sue wrote in her memo book, "Refill paper loader—1500." That was all she needed to write down. That was the most important information.

Activity A: Let's see how good you are at writing down the most important ideas. Below are some *oral* or spoken directions that you might get on one of the first days of a job. Read them carefully. Then, on a separate sheet of paper, write down the key words or ideas. Write what you would need to help you remember the oral directions.

"When the mail comes in, the first thing you want to do is sort it according to office. You'll find a list of the offices in the company directory that is on the counter right there. After the mail is sorted, you deliver the mail. The first mail you deliver is to Mr. Brewster, the president. After that the order doesn't matter. Don't linger. All the mail should be delivered in twenty minutes. See this mail sheet? The secretary in each office must initial it when you deliver the mail. Bring that sheet back with you and put it in the file under 'Mail Sheets.' Put it in the front of the file right in front of the last one."

Summary

It is not hard to see that Sue made a good start at her new job. She was careful to get paperwork done correctly. She asked questions when she had to learn what to do. She read and followed written directions carefully. When oral directions were given, she took notes to help her remember what was being said.

You will want to do as well as Sue when you start a new job. Practicing the skills you learned in this chapter will help you to follow directions. Complete the activities in the Chapter Review for more practice.

CHAPTER REVIEW

Review Activity A: Shown below is a time card. On a separate sheet of paper, number from 1 to 4. Write the information that would be filled in next to each number.

The Hall Distribution Company
EMPLOYEE TIME CARD

(1)
_____
Employee's Name   (print)

(2)
_____
For Week Beginning

(3)
_____
Social Security Number

(4)
_____
Employee's Signature

Review Activity B: Given below is a set of directions. On a separate piece of paper, make a schedule from these directions.

1. Turn off electric typewriter if you leave your desk for longer than fifteen minutes.
2. Dust typewriter before turning machine on every day.
3. Clean keys, elements, etc., once a week.
4. Cover typewriter at the end of each day.
5. Clean underside of typewriter once a week.
6. All typewriters should have professional cleaning at least once a year.
7. If your typewriter needs repairs, call 555-8847.

Review Activity C: Study the work schedule below. Then decide if the statements under the schedule are true or false. On a separate sheet of paper, number from 1 to 8. If the statement is true, write *True* next to the number. If it is not true, write *False*.

WORK SCHEDULE

Employee	Starting Time
Anderson, Leo	7:30 a.m.
Clay, Jennie	8:00 a.m.
Eakins, Joe	8:30 a.m.
Green, Hazel	9:00 a.m.
Harris, Nathan	9:30 a.m.

This week each employee is asked to put in one hour of overtime each day.

---

1. The company staggers the time its employees arrive at work and leave work.

2. No one will work overtime.

3. Leo Anderson gets to work two hours earlier than Hazel Green.

4. Leo Anderson will leave work two hours earlier than Nathan Harris.

5. No two employees arrive and leave at the same time.

6. Even though each employee will work one hour overtime each day, they will still leave and arrive at different times.

7. If the employees normally put in an $8^1/_2$-hour day, Jennie Clay would leave work at 4:30 p.m.

8. If she worked an hour overtime, Hazel would leave work at 7 p.m.

Review Activity D: Given below are some oral directions. Read them carefully. Then, on a separate sheet of paper, write down the key words or ideas. Write what you would need to help you remember the oral directions.

"Here are some things to remember about using this grill. First, wipe it with cooking oil before you turn it on. Set it at 'middle high' for everything but fried potatoes. Set it at 'high' for them. Every time you cook something, scrape the grill with the scraper and reoil the grill. Cook onions over in the far-left corner of the grill. That way they won't make everything else smell. When the crowd ends and you don't have to cook, turn the grill down to 'medium low.' If you turn it lower than that, it will take too long to heat back up if a customer comes in. When you leave at the end of the day, you make sure that the grill is clean, and I mean clean!"

Review Activity E: Read the oral directions above. Then, on a separate sheet of paper, answer these questions.

1. At what temperature do you cook eggs?

2. At what temperature do you cook potatoes?

3. Why should onions be cooked in the far-left corner of the grill?

4. If you turn the grill down too low, what will happen when a customer comes in?

5. Whose responsibility is cleaning the grill?

6. What must the grill cook do each time after he cooks something?

CHAPTER 9

Learning More Job Skills

Thomas Tyler had been working on his new job for six months. He liked the work and was doing well. Because Tom got along so well with his supervisors and fellow workers, the bosses decided that they would give Tom a *promotion*. The new job that they wanted Tom to take would mean that he would have to use trade manuals and be able to read all kinds of graphs, charts, and labels. Tom was glad to be promoted, but he was worried. He had not yet had the training to do those things.

Tom decided to turn down the promotion. When he explained to his boss why he was turning it down, Mr. Barber said, "Oh, Tom, don't worry. We plan to send you to school for the first week you are in the new job. Then you can learn all the things that you will need to know."

Tom was relieved. The school he was going to attend was held right at the factory. It was run by supervisors who knew exactly what Tom had to know to do a good job. At the end of the week, Tom felt he had learned everything he needed to know. He felt ready for the promotion.

Lesson 1: Using Trade Manuals

The first thing Tom was taught was how to use, read, and understand trade manuals. *Trade manuals* are books about certain skilled jobs like plumbing or electrical work. These manuals can explain how to do certain jobs. They can describe new tools or methods or products in the trade, and so on.

Mr. Barber's company is a plumbing company, so the trade manuals that Tom was given to read were plumbing manuals. Here is a section of a plumbing trade manual about water heaters. Read it carefully.

> The acceptable temperature for domestic hot water is from 140 to 160 degrees Fahrenheit. If an automatic clothes washer or dishwasher is in use, 160 degrees is preferred. Temperatures above 160 degrees are not recommended. They cause increased corrosion, increased deposit of lime, waste of fuel, more rapid heat loss by radiation, danger of scalding, and other accidents.

As you read, you probably realized that this is helpful information about setting the temperature of a hot water heater. The instructions are meant for the plumber who is installing a water heater. Notice that the plumber has several questions to consider when he decides on the correct temperature.

• Does this family have a clothes washer?

• Does this family have a dishwasher?

The manual also gives the plumber reasons why he should not set a water heater above 160 degrees. Do you know what those reasons are? Look in the last sentence of the paragraph from the manual.

Activity A: Now try to read a part of a trade manual by yourself. Then answer the following questions on a separate sheet of paper.

> Globe valves have a machined seat and a composition disc and usually shut off tight, while gate valves may leak slightly when closed, particularly if frequently operated, due to wear between the brass gates and the faces against which they operate. Globe valves create more flow resistance than gate valves.

1. Which valve will shut off tighter?
2. What causes a gate valve to leak?
3. Which valve creates more flow resistance?
4. Suppose you were Tom and you had to pick a valve for a job. You do not want leaking. Which valve would you choose?
5. Which valve has a machined seat and a composition disc?
6. Why do you think that frequent operation would cause a gate valve to leak?
7. Suppose you were Tom and you had to pick a valve for a job. You want the least flow resistance possible. Which valve would you choose?
8. Two kinds of valves are compared in this portion of the trade manual. What are they?

Manuals Describing New Materials

On the next page is a part of a trade manual that describes new plumbing products. Read it to see if Tom should recommend this product.

The new Rxt supply valves, manufactured by Friendly Plumbing Corp., are available in both straight and angle configurations. They will adapt to copper tubing, as well as plastic tubing and conventional flexible chrome-plated copper supply tubes. The compression-type connections can be installed without the use of wrenches; they represent a vast improvement over conventional brass supply valves.

The Rxt supply valve is a new product. Let's see if you can answer some questions about it.

Activity B: On a separate sheet of paper, number from 1 to 7. Then read the following statements. If the statement is true, write *True* next to the number of the statement. If the statement is not true, write *False* next to the number.

1. These new supply valves are manufactured by Rxt Supply Company.
2. You can get these new valves for straight or for angle shapes.
3. They will not adapt to copper tubing.
4. They will adapt to plastic tubing.
5. You need a wrench to install these valves.
6. The new Rxt supply valves are much better than brass supply valves.
7. The Friendly Plumbing Corporation, which manufactures the Rxt supply valve, has made them in two shapes.

Lesson 2: The Index Is Important

Tom found that in order to get the best use from a manual or instruction book, he had to know how to read the *index*. Sometimes reading such a list could be tricky. Remember, Tom was reading about valves. He wanted more information. This is what he found in the index.

> Valve seat dresser, 7, 10
> Valve seat wrench, 7, 10
> Valves, 4, 26

Where do you think he would have to look for "supply valves"? Probably he can find information on either page 4 or page 26.

Activity A: Some indexes use capital letters to indicate *major headings*. Let's see how well you can interpret an index. On a separate sheet of paper, answer the following questions about this sample index.

> Aluminum welding, 66-67
> Arbor press, 498
> Arc welding, 70-80
>   accessories, 73-74
>   electrode classification, 71
>   electrodes, 71
>   freezing of the electrode, 75-76
>   machines, 74
>   operations and uses, 72-74
>   protection equipment, 73
>   starting the arc, 75-77
> Arcing, 534-545

1. What two kinds of welding can you find in the book?
2. Are arcing and arc welding the same thing? How can you tell?
3. Do you need protection equipment for arc welding?
4. On what pages would you find out how to start the arc?

Activity B: Read the sample index below. Then, on a separate sheet of paper, answer the following questions about this index.

Applications, 326-366
    credit, 345
    educational, 328, 347
    financial, 365
    job, 333
    permits, 357
    work benefits, 360
Area codes, 214-218
Catalogs, 127-198
    business, 134
    mail order, 144-168

1. How many major headings are included in this portion of an index? What are they?
2. If you wanted to find out something about an application for a building permit, on which page would you look?
3. If you wanted to find out what area codes were and how they are used, on which pages would you look?
4. If you were applying for a credit card and wanted some help filling out the application, on what page would you look?
5. If you wanted some information about ordering from a mail order catalog, on what pages would you look?
6. In order to get information about using business catalogs, on what page would you look?
7. Does this book appear to have information in it about using the atlas?
8. If you wanted to fill in an application for college, where in this book would you look?
9. You wish to make an application for a loan from your bank. You need help. On which page of this book would you look?

Lesson 3: Reading Charts and Graphs

Being able to read and interpret graphs and charts was another important part of Tom's new job. He had to be able to understand production charts, quota charts, and other work-related charts. A *chart* is a diagram that presents information in table or list form.

One of the charts that Tom had to read each month was the production chart. This chart was especially important because it identified which shop was responsible for how much production for that month.

Production Chart ... March, 1995			
Section	Deluxe Model	Budget Model	Hotel and Office Model
Tubs	146	278	539
Toilets	512	1036	5427
Wash Basins	448	795	968
Showers	90	40	720
	For all of the above listed:		
Fittings	1196	2149	7654

Notice that each section is named for the product that it produces—tubs, toilets, and so on. Notice that the company makes three models of each product—deluxe, budget, and one for hotels and offices. The fittings section makes all the additional parts (handles, drains, and so forth) for all models of all products.

Activity A: On a separate sheet of paper, answer these questions.
1. According to the chart, how many deluxe bathtubs were made?
2. How many showers were made?
3. Why does the fittings section have to know what all the other sections are doing?

Bar Graphs

A *bar graph* is a diagram that uses lines and shaded areas to present and compare information. This graph shows the percentage of products sent back to the company because they were faulty. The company wants to improve this record. Tom studied this graph carefully.

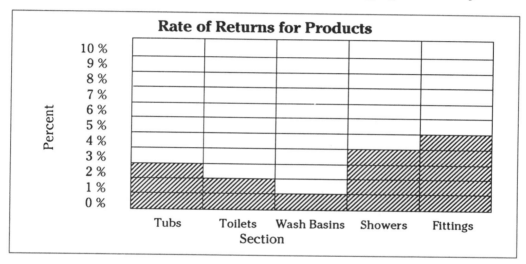

Tom noticed that the wash basin section had the fewest returns. He also noticed that fittings had the most returns. Since they had to work with the smallest parts and with the most working parts, that large number of returns made sense.

Activity B: Write *True* or *False* for each statement below.

1. The wash basin section had less than 1% return.
2. The shower section had 4% return.
3. The tub section had a 20% return.
4. The fittings section had the most merchandise returned.
5. This graph could show up to a 10% return.

Lesson 4: Reading Labels to Get What You Need

Part of Tom Tyler's new job would include getting stock from the stock room. At the training program, instructors taught him how to read and interpret the labels on packages so that he could tell what he was getting from the stock room. *Labels* are words or abbreviations attached to objects in order to identify or describe them.

The first thing Tom had to do was learn some abbreviations commonly found on labels. These abbreviations dealt with size, number, material, and color. Look at Tom's list.

LABEL ABBREVIATIONS

Size
sm.　— small
lg.　— large
med. — medium

Number
doz. — dozen
gr.　— gross　(12 dozen)
rm.　— ream　(500 sheets)

Material
st.　— steel
cop. — copper
plas. — plastic
pap. — paper

Color
blk. — black
wh.　— white
yel. — yellow

Activity A: Look at Tom's list of label abbreviations. Then look at the labels below. On a separate sheet of paper, rewrite these labels. Change each abbreviation to the word it stands for.

1. Plas. Tubing sm. 2 doz. lengths wh.

2. Pap. Wallboard 1 gr. yel.

Summary

For many jobs, you need skills that most people don't even think about. Many jobs require that a worker be able to read and understand trade manuals. Some of these manuals are very technical and describe special trades and skills. They have difficult language. Trade manuals have to be read carefully and have to be understood. Your job may depend on it. Some trade manuals explain how to do a job or procedure. Others tell you about new products that may be better than the ones you are using.

In order to use these trade manuals as well as possible, you need to be able to read and understand an index. An index, usually at the back of a book, tells you the pages on which you can find certain information.

Some jobs require that you read and understand graphs and charts. Charts and graphs can give you information in a quick, easy-to-see way.

You must also be able to read and understand labels on many jobs. Selecting the wrong material because you couldn't understand the label can cost money and time and can even cost you your job.

While all of the above skills vary from job to job, it is important that you have some practice. Then you will be ready if the time comes when you need to be able to read and understand manuals, indexes, charts, graphs, and labels. Once you are working, you will pick up the exact skills you need faster.

CHAPTER REVIEW

Review Activity A: Read this entry from a trade manual. Then, on a separate sheet of paper, answer the following questions.

Directions to Set Electrical Timer

Slide one control tab completely out, toward the edge of the dial, for each hour of "on" time you want. Sliding out tab between 5:00 p.m. and 6:00 p.m. will turn on appliance for one hour beginning at 5:00 p.m. If you desire longer period of time, slide out additional control tabs.

---

1.   What are these directions for?
2.   If you slide one control tab out, how long will the appliance operate?
3.   In which direction should the tab be pushed to be "out"?
4.   If you want the appliance to run for more than one hour, what should you do?

Review Activity B: Shown below is part of an index. On your own paper, write the answers to the questions at the top of the next page.

Counters, 74-90
    building, 74-80
    installation, 80-85
    measurement, 74-78
    tops, 85-90
Drains, 55-73
    appliance, 72
    fixture, 55-60
    floor, 60
    unstopping, 61-64

Questions about the index:

1. Does this book give information on installing counters?
2. On what pages can you look to find out about measuring counters?
3. If you want to build a counter yourself, on what pages would you look?
4. What three kinds of drains are discussed in this book?
5. If you want to read the whole section on drains, what pages would you read?
6. If you want to find out how to unstop a drain, on what pages would you look?
7. If you want to replace a counter top, where would you look?

Review Activity C: Read the entry below carefully. This entry is taken from a trade journal advertising a new product. Then look at the following statements. Number your own paper from 1 to 6. If the statement is true, write *True*. If the statement is not true, write *False*.

> The new three-pane window can be removed easily to be cleaned. It has heavy-duty, smooth-operating sash balance, full weather-stripped interlock, insulated glass, and a movable outside screen. The frame is made of vinyl and guaranteed for five years.

1. This new window has two panes of glass.
2. It is easy to remove.
3. The frame is made of vinyl.
4. The sash balance is lightweight.
5. The interlock is weather-stripped.
6. It is not guaranteed.

Review Activity D: Shown below is a chart of prices for kitchen cabinets. Study this chart. Then answer the following questions. Write your answers on your own paper.

Wooden Kitchen Cabinets				
	5'	6'	7'	8'
Light Pine	$547	$602	$772	$907
Dark Pine	$547	$602	$772	$907
Light Oak	$555	$614	$791	$932
Dark Oak	$555	$614	$791	$932

1. What is the longest cabinet listed on this chart?

2. Which cabinets are more expensive—oak or pine?

3. If you wanted to buy a 7' kitchen cabinet of light oak, how much would you pay for it?

4. How much would you pay for an 8' light pine cabinet?

5. How much more expensive is a 5' light oak cabinet than a 5' light pine cabinet?

Review Activity E: Study the graph below. Number from 1 to 10 on a separate sheet of paper. Then read the following statements. If the statement is true, write *True* next to the number of the statement. If it is not true, write *False*.

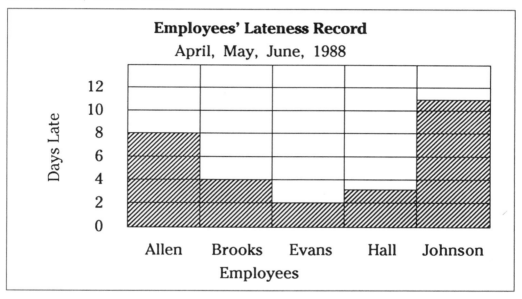

Employees' Lateness Record

April, May, June, 1988

1. This chart shows how many times workers were late.
2. The chart covers a period of one year.
3. No worker was late twelve days.
4. Brooks was late four days.
5. Evans was never late.
6. Hall was late only one day.
7. Johnson was on time except for ten days.
8. Allen had the best record for coming to work on time.
9. Hall had the worst record for coming to work on time.
10. Brooks and Hall were late the same number of days.

Review Activity F: On a separate sheet of paper, number from 1 to 12. Match the abbreviation in the first column with the correct meaning in the second column. Write the letter of the correct meaning next to the number of each abbreviation.

Abbreviation	**Meaning**
1. pap.	a. yellow
2. med.	b. white
3. rm.	c. black
4. yel.	d. small
5. lg.	e. large
6. plas.	f. medium
7. wh.	g. steel
8. gr.	h. copper
9. cop.	i. plastic
10. doz.	j. paper
11. blk.	k. dozen
12. st.	l. gross—12 dozen
	m. ream—500 sheets

Review Activity G: Choose a word from the box to complete each sentence correctly. Write your answers on a separate sheet of paper.

products	manuals	books
do	describe	

1. Trade _____ are_____ about certain jobs or skills.
2. They give instructions or explain how to_____ certain jobs.
3. They can also_____ new_____ .

CHAPTER 10

Filling Out
Business Forms

George Hill worked for Y. Little Office Supplies as a sales clerk. His friend, Myra York, worked for the same company in the stock department. Y. Little Office Supplies is a large company with five stores in the Memphis, Tennessee, area.

George sells office supplies either to people who come in off the street to buy items or to people who call in orders. Myra works with the *inventories* in all five stores. She lists the amount of goods or materials on hand. She has to make sure that each store has enough stock and the right stock. She has to order new stock when amounts get low.

Both George and Myra have to fill out several kinds of forms. Myra also has to be able to write letters to order stock items and to follow up on orders. These workers can not do a good job if they cannot fill out the required forms correctly.

Lesson 1: Sales Slips

George and Myra often talk together about their work and compare their jobs. Let's learn about their work and compare what they do. We will begin by looking at George's job. After a customer has selected the items he or she wishes to purchase, George must write an accurate *sales slip*. He must keep a copy of this form so that Y. Little & Company has a record of who bought what, how much they paid, and when they made the purchase.

Shown below is the kind of sales slip that George must complete.

Y. Little & Company
14 South Street
Memphis, Tennessee 38101

Date *March 17, 1996*

Sold to *John Murray*

Address *2736 Natchez Place*

City, State ZIP *Memphis, TN 38113*

How Many	Item #	Description	Unit Price	Amount
5	9738	*Legal pads*	*$3.00*	*$15.00*
1 box	7638	*Butterfly clips*	*5.00*	*5.00*
1	1121	*Name stamps*	*8.00*	*8.00*
			Subtotal	*$28.00*
			Sales Tax	*2.17*
			Total	*$30.17*

Notice how neatly and carefully George has filled out this sales slip. He supplied the date, customer's name, address, city, and ZIP code.

Below that information are five columns. The first column asks, "How many?" The second column asks for an *item number*. It is used to identify each separate item sold by a company. George had to get that item number from the label on the item or from a catalog printed by his company. Then, in the third column, he had to describe what the item was.

The price for each item had to be written in the fourth column. That column contains the price of only one unit of each item. Sometimes this *unit price* is for each box, each dozen, each gallon, etc., rather than for each single item. Notice that Mr. Murray bought five legal pads. George had to multiply $3.00 by 5 (the unit price x the number purchased) to get the *amount* in the last column. That total cost for pads is $15.00. Mr. Murray bought only one box of butterfly clips and one name stamp, so George did not have to multiply to get those amounts.

After George listed everything Mr. Murray bought, he added the amounts in the last column to get the *subtotal*. In Memphis a customer has to pay 7.75% tax on goods sold. George had to figure the amount for *sales tax*. The subtotal of $28.00 x 7.75% = $2.17. Finally, he added the subtotal and the tax to get the *total* ($30.17) for Mr. Murray's bill.

George checked his arithmetic twice to make sure that Mr. Murray's bill was correct. He also checked to make sure that he had copied the item numbers correctly. A sales slip is an important record for the store and for the customer. George's boss does not like his salespeople to make mistakes. Those mistakes make customers angry and can cost a company money. George has learned to be very careful.

Activity A: This sales slip was not filled in correctly. Study it carefully. On a sheet of paper, list the 14 mistakes made in filling out this sales slip.

Y. Little & Company
14 South Street
Memphis, Tennessee 38101

Date _____

Sold to _Phillips_ _____

Address _Calhoun Ave._ _____

City, State ZIP _Memphis_ _____

How Many	Item #	Description	Unit Price	Amount
3	9711	Typing paper		$12.51
6		Correction fluid	1.00	6.00
2	8321			7.00
4	9101	Memo pads	1.25	6.00
3	4320	Liquid adhesive	3.00	9.15
			Subtotal	$50.76
			Sales Tax	1.75
			Total	$52.41

Lesson 2: Invoices

George also filled out an invoice. This form is much like a sales slip. An *invoice* contains a list of goods sold; it gives the price of each item and the terms of sale. George used the invoice for customers who had accounts with Y. Little & Company. They paid their bills every month instead of at the time of each sale. Study the invoice on page 163.

Y. Little & Company
14 South Street
Memphis, Tennessee 38101

- Office Supplies
- Printing
- Office Furniture

DELIVER TO

If delivery address is different from shown below, fill in above

BILL TO
Franklin N. Brussells
2345 Beech Street
Memphis, Tennessee 38024

| Invoice Number 591006 |
| Date *4 - 1 - 96* |
| Customer Order Number *37 - 24* |
| Ordered by *Smith* |
| Sold by *Hill* |
| Audit |

√	Quantity Ordered	Quantity Delivered	Unit of Sale	Description	Unit Price	Per	Amount
	2	*2*	*dz.*	*948 Pads*	*$12.00*	*dz.*	*$24.00*
				Less 15%			*3.60*
					Subtotal		*$20.40*

| Service Charge of 1¹/₂% per month, 18% per annum, will be applied to all 60 day old balances. | Sales Tax | *1.58* |
| Received above items in good condition | Regular stock merchandise can be returned for exchange credit or refund if in perfect condition and if returned within 30 days of date of purchase. | Total | *$21.98* |

At the top left is a space for the name and address of the person to whom the goods are to be delivered. Notice that George writes this information only if the delivery address differs from the billing address. (The direction says: "If delivery address is different from shown below, fill in above.") On the right is the invoice number, printed on the form. Below is a place for the date, customer order number, name of the person who ordered goods, and name of the salesperson who made the sale. Information about ordered items is listed on the appropriate lines.

One copy of the invoice goes to the customer for his or her records. Another copy is kept by the salesperson. A third copy would go to the billing department. The last copy would go to the inventory department.

Activity A: Study the invoice below. Then, on a separate sheet of paper, answer the questions below this invoice.

• Office Supplies • Printing • Office Furniture		**Y. Little & Company** **14 South Street** **Memphis, Tennessee 38101**				

D
E
L
I TO   *Standard Wharf*
V   *11 Murphy Street*
E   *38170*
R

If delivery address is different from shown below, fill in above

B
I TO   *Standard Company*
L   *4627 Dale Street*
L   *38181*

Invoice Number 591038
Date *5 - 6 - 96*
Customer Order Number *4961*
Ordered by *Brad*
Sold by *Hill*
Audit

√	Quantity Ordered	Quantity Delivered	Unit of Sale	Description	Unit Price	Per	Amount
	1	*1*	*ea.*	*B64 Desk*	*$175.15*	*ea.*	*$175.15*
√	*2*	*1*	*ea.*	*N77 Desk Chair*	*45.00*	*ea.*	*90.00*
							265.15
				Less 15%			*39.77*
√	*Other chair will follow*					Subtotal	*$225.38*

Service Charge of 1¹/₂% per month, 18% per annum, will be applied to all 60 day old balances.   **Sales Tax**   *17.47*

Received above items in good condition   Regular stock merchandise can be returned for exchange credit or refund if in perfect condition and if returned within 30 days of date of purchase.   **Total**   *$242.85*

1. Where will the furniture be delivered?
2. Why is the furniture being delivered to some place other than where the bill is to be sent?
3. Who ordered the furniture?
4. How many desks were ordered and delivered?
5. How much did the desk cost?
6. How many chairs were ordered and delivered?
7. How much did the chairs cost?
8. Why do you think that only one chair was delivered?
9. What was the cost of the furniture before the discount and the tax?

Lesson 3: Keeping Inventory Records

After George and the other salespeople fill out sales slips, copies are sent to Myra's department. She and her fellow workers check off what items have been sold from the inventory. The inventory is a list of what goods or materials Y. Little and Company have on hand. Subtracting from inventory tells the workers what items are left in stock and what inventory items may be running low.

When stock is sold and only a certain amount is left, the people in Myra's office know that it is time to reorder that item. The amount of any item that can safely be left at reorder time is decided ahead of time. It is based on how popular that item is, how fast it sells, how long it will take to get more, and so on.

Y. Little & Company, like most businesses, uses computers to keep its inventory. Every day, as copies of the sales slips arrive in her office, Myra enters the items that have been sold into the computer. If she needs to know which store is selling how much of what, the *computer printout* can tell her.

You may remember that on March 17, 1996, George sold John Murray one box of butterfly clips. Myra has entered that item on the computer. Since George works at the main store, that box of clips would be included in the total number of boxes of clips the store sold that day.

When Myra has compiled the information, she may get a printout from the computer. This printed record is produced automatically by a computer. A sample computer printout is shown on top of the next page.

Boxes Sold
Butterfly Clips

Date	Main Store	Plaza	3rd St.	Opera	Fine St.
3/15	92	5	12	8	7
3/16	56	4	10	11	6
3/17	71	10	5	9	3

This listing tells how many boxes of butterfly clips were sold in each of the five stores on three days. Included in the 71 boxes sold at the main store on March 17 is the one box that George sold to Mr. Murray.

These figures have been entered into company files. Then the computer can give Myra information about the company's stock of butterfly clips.

Item: Butterfly clips		Reorder below: 500 boxes
3/10	In stock — 1050 boxes	
3/13	to Main Store — 510 boxes	
	Remainder — 540	
3/14	to Plaza Store — 35 boxes	
	Remainder — 505 boxes	
3/14	to 3rd St. Store — 10 boxes	
	Remainder — 495 boxes	REORDER
3/14	Ordered 2016	
3/21	Received order	
	Total — 2511	

Myra can tell from the information given to her by the computer that on March 10 the company had 1,050 boxes of butterfly clips on hand. Because the main store was getting low on butterfly clips, they were sent 510 boxes on March 13. The Plaza Store was sent 35 boxes the next day, and the 3rd St. Store got 10 boxes. These figures meant that only 495 boxes of butterfly clips were left in inventory.

Next to the figure 495 on the printout, the computer has printed the word "REORDER." Can you figure out why? Look at the top of the information sheet. When does it say to reorder? If you said, "Below 500 boxes," you were correct.

On March 14, Myra ordered 2,016 boxes of butterfly clips. Can you figure out when that order was delivered? If you said, "March 21," you were correct.

Activity A: Shown below is a computer printout that gives some inventory information about correction fluid. Study this inventory information. Then answer the following questions on another sheet of paper.

```
Item: Correction fluid              Reorder below: 30 doz. bot.
3/10        In stock — 76 dozen bot.
3/10        to Fine St. Store — 10 doz. bot.
            Remainder — 66 doz. bot.
3/14        to Opera Store — 12 doz. bot.
            Remainder — 54 doz. bot.
3/15        to Main Store — 20 doz. bot.
            Remainder — 34 doz. bot.
```

1. Did Myra have to reorder correction fluid from March 10 through March 15? Why or why not?
2. How many bottles of correction fluid were in stock at the close of the day on March 10?
3. Why do you think there is no entry for March 13?
4. How many bottles of correction fluid were sent to the Main Store? When were they sent?

Lesson 4: Using Catalogs

When Myra had to reorder butterfly clips, she had to use the *catalog* put out by the paper clip company. She had to be able to read the catalog descriptions to tell which kind of clip she wanted. It was very important that Myra not make a mistake. If she ordered the wrong thing, several problems could occur. First, her company would be stuck with something they did not want. Second, her company would not have enough butterfly clips to sell to their own customers.

Here is the section of the catalog that Myra used to make her order. In this case the unit price is for each gross, not each box.

Clips			
#5566 — paper	100 per box	$5.78	per gross
#5567 — paper	500 per box	$20.11	per gross
#5580 — butterfly	50 per box	$4.90	per gross
#5581 — butterfly	100 per box	$9.20	per gross

Myra knew that the clips she needed to reorder came 100 per box. Which item number would she order? If you said, "Number 5581," you were correct. How many boxes are in a gross? If you said, "Twelve dozen boxes, or 144 boxes," you were correct.

If Myra had ordered item #5566, she would have gotten paper clips. They would not have been what she needed. Look at these two drawings. The top drawing shows a paper clip. The bottom drawing shows a butterfly clip. Why do you think a customer who wanted butterfly clips could not use paper clips? If you said that butterfly clips hold greater amounts of paper together, you were correct.

Activity A: Shown below is a group of entries from a supply catalog. Study them carefully. Then, on a separate sheet of paper, number from 1 to 8. If the statement is true, write *True* next to the number of the statement. If the statement is not true, write *False*.

Pens		
Ballpoint,	throaway	**$7.70** doz.
Ballpoint,	refillable	**$11.55** doz.
Ballpoint,	retractable throaway	**$10.45** doz.
Ballpoint,	retractable refillable	**$14.33** doz.

1. Four kinds of ballpoint pens are listed in this catalog entry.

2. The lowest price is for ballpoint pens with retractable points that you can throw away.

3. You cannot buy refillable pens that do not have retractable points.

4. Ballpoint pens that are refillable and that have retractable points are the most expensive pens.

5. Businesses that provide pens for their employees or customers would probably buy throwaway pens without retractable points because they have the lowest price.

6. Two dozen ballpoint pens that have retractable points but that cannot be refilled would cost $24.90.

7. The throwaway ballpoint pens without retractable tips cost about 64¢ each.

8. The refillable ballpoint pens with retractable tips cost about $1.19 each.

Lesson 5: Writing an Order Letter

Part of Myra's job is writing *order letters* to order merchandise. Not all items are ordered by mail. Some are ordered over the telephone or by fax machine. Such orders are particularly common if it is a rush order. However, most businesses prefer to order by mail. The letter gives them a record of what they have ordered and when it was ordered. If companies are sent the wrong item, they simply refer to their copy of the letter to prove to the seller what they actually did order.

Because letters ordering merchandise are so important, Myra has to have a great deal of skill. She needs to write letters that contain all the information needed to receive the correct items.

For example, if Myra had written a letter ordering butterfly clips, she would have included the following information in the body of her order letter:

- the billing/shipping address;
- the item number from the catalog of the company from which she is ordering;
- a description of the item;
- the unit or individual price of the item;
- the number of units she is ordering;
- the subtotal of those units, sales tax, and total cost;
- the way in which Y. Little & Company will pay for the merchandise;
- the delivery method preferred; and
- the date when she must have the merchandise.

Myra must check the rough drafts of her letters to make sure that all the correct information is included.

Activity A: Shown below is a rough draft of the order letter Myra wrote. Read it carefully. Then, on a separate sheet of paper, list any information she left out. Use the list on the previous page to help you.

Y. Little & Company
14 South Street
Memphis, Tennessee 38101

March 14, 1996

Arlington Clip Company
6500 Wright Avenue
Trenton, New Jersey 08608

Attention: Robert Michael

Dear Mr. Michael:

Please ship to the above address 14 gross of butterfly clips, 100 per box, at a cost of $9.20 per gross.

Thank you for your cooperation.

Very truly yours,

Myra York

Myra York
Stock Department

Activity B: Suppose you wanted to order 10 dozen reams of erasable bond paper, measuring $8\frac{1}{2}$" by 11". Suppose you wanted the company to send you a bill. On your own paper, write an order letter. Make up the address of the company from which you are ordering. Add any other needed information to your order letter. Use the list on the previous page to help you.

Lesson 6: Correcting Mistakes

No matter how careful Myra and her coworkers are, sometimes a mistake is made in an order. Sometimes the order does not arrive, or contains the wrong merchandise, or has not enough or too much of what is ordered. Then Myra has to write a *follow-up letter* to get the mistake corrected.

This kind of letter must be especially clear. It must explain the problem clearly and politely. It must explain what Myra's company wants done about the mistake. Mistakes can cost Y. Little & Company money and can also make them lose customers. If a customer cannot get what he or she wants from Y. Little & Company, that customer will take his or her business somewhere else.

When Myra writes a follow-up letter, she must include some of the information she included in the earlier order letter as well as some other information. She must include:

- the item number from the catalog of the company from which she is ordering;
- a description of the item;
- the unit or individual price of the item;
- the number of units she ordered;
- the subtotal cost of those units, sales tax, and total cost;
- the copies of necessary bills, invoices, etc.;
- an explanation of the problem; and
- the steps she would like taken to solve this problem.

As in ordering merchandise, Myra must check the rough drafts of her follow-up letters carefully to make sure that all the information is included and is correct.

Activity A: Below is the rough draft of Myra's follow-up letter. Read it carefully. Then, on a separate sheet of paper, list any information she should have included in this letter. Use the list on page 172 to help you.

Y. Little & Company
14 South Street
Memphis, Tennessee 38101

March 23, 1996

Arlington Clip Company
6500 Wright Avenue
Trenton, New Jersey 08608

Attention: Robert Michael

Dear Mr. Michael:

On March 14 I ordered from your company 14 gross of butterfly clips, 100 per box, at the cost of $9.20 per gross. The item number for those clips is #5581.

On March 21 I received from you 14 gross of butterfly clips, 50 per box, for which Y. Little & Company was charged $9.20 per gross. Attached is a copy of the invoice sent with this order.

Please send us the correct merchandise immediately. Credit our account with the original order that we shipped back to you today. We must have the correct order by March 31 in order to keep enough stock in our inventory.

I would appreciate your immediate attention to this matter.

Very truly yours,

Myra York
Stock Department

Summary

Many different forms are used by businesses. Two of the most frequently used forms are the sales slip and the invoice. These forms must be filled out carefully in order to give both the customer and the company accurate information about what was bought when and how much was paid for it.

Sales slips and invoices are used to help companies keep track of the inventory they have. A well-kept inventory makes it possible for companies never to run out of important items that they need to operate their businesses.

At some time, you may be working at a job that requires you to order supplies and equipment for your company. You must know how to use order catalogs so that you are sure of ordering the correct item.

Many orders for supplies and materials are made through the use of the business letter. It is helpful for an employee to know business letter form and to know what information must be included in a letter ordering supplies.

Sometimes incorrect orders are received. Then the employee must know how to write a good follow-up letter explaining what the problem is and describing how this problem should be corrected.

Being able to fill out a form correctly, to read a computer printout, and to write good letters are skills that are important to many jobs. Knowing these skills can help you to get ahead in the world of business.

CHAPTER REVIEW

Review Activity A: Shown below is a sales slip. It is not filled in correctly. Study it carefully. On another sheet of paper, list the seven mistakes made by the person filling out this sales slip.

Y. Little & Company
14 South Street
Memphis, Tennessee 38101

Date *3 / 20 / 96*

Sold to *Mary Green*

Address *1230 North Bend Road*

City, State ZIP *Memphis*

How Many	Item #	Description	Unit Price	Amount
1	5420	Desk blotter		$ .75
1	4186	Calendar	$3.25	3.25
2	3970	Letter basket	5.60	11.20
1		File envelopes	7.50	7.50
				$32.60
			Subtotal	
			Sales Tax	
			Total	$32.60

Review Activity B: On a separate sheet of paper, list the things a good salesperson should do to fill out a sales slip correctly and to make sure that all the information on the form is right.

Review Activity C: Shown below is an invoice. Study it carefully.

1. This invoice is not filled out correctly. On another sheet of paper, list the eight mistakes made by the person who filled out the invoice.

2. Answer these questions about the invoice. Use your own paper.
    a. Why is the date of this purchase important?
    b. Is this a cash sale or a charge sale? How do you know?
    c. There is no address for Spirl, Inc. What extra work could this cause the billing department?
    d. There is no information about how many items were delivered. What kinds of problems might this cause?
    e. The "Deliver To" section is blank. Why isn't this a mistake?

Review Activity D: Shown below is some computer information about an inventory. Study it carefully. Then, on a separate sheet of paper, answer the following questions.

Item: Pens, Ballpoint, throw-away   Reorder below: 10 doz.
4/16   In stock — 115 doz.
              to Plaza Store — 10 doz.
              to Fine St. Store — 20 doz.
              Remainder — 85 doz.
4/17   to Main Store — 50 doz.
              Remainder — 35 doz.

1. For what merchandise is this an inventory?

2. When does the stock department need to reorder this merchandise?

3. How many ballpoint pens were in stock at the beginning of the day on April 16?

4. On April 16, what stores were sent ballpoint pens?

5. How many ballpoint pens were in stock at the end of the day on April 16?

6. How many ballpoint pens were sent to the Main Store? When were they sent?

7. How many ballpoint pens were in stock at the end of the day on April 17?

8. How many days are shown in this entry?

Review Activity E: Shown below is an entry from a supply catalog. Study it carefully.   Then, on a separate sheet of paper, answer the following questions.

Paper — $8^1/_2$ x 11		
Bond, erasable	**$15.00**	per ream
Bond, nonerasable	**$12.25**	per ream
Bond, ripple erasable	**$18.00**	per ream

1. How many different kinds of paper are listed in this entry?

2. What size is the paper?

3. How much does one ream of bond ripple erasable paper cost?

4. What is the least expensive kind of paper in this entry?

5. If you wanted to purchase ten reams of bond nonerasable, how much would it cost?

6. If you ordered two reams of bond nonerasable and four reams of bond ripple erasable, what would your total bill be?

Review Activity F: Write an order letter to Phillips Paper Company. Order 7 reams of $8^1/_2$" by 11" bond ripple erasable paper that costs $18.00 per ream. Phillips Paper Company is located on 115 Howard Street, Newark, Delaware 19711. You are enclosing a check for the total cost of the paper. You do not have to pay sales tax.

Hint: Check the list Myra used to write her order letter. This list can be found on page 170 of the text. You may add any other information needed to make this order letter complete.

Review Activity G: The Phillips Paper Company sent you 7 reams of $8^{1}/_{2}$" by 14" bond erasable paper instead of what you ordered in Review Activity F. Write them a follow-up letter explaining their mistake and telling what you want them to do to correct it.

Hint: Check the list Myra used to write her follow-up letter. This list can be found on page 172 of the text. You may add any other information needed to make this follow-up letter complete.

Review Activity H: On a separate sheet of paper, number from 1 to 8. Then read the following statements. If the statement is true, write *True* next to the number of the statement. If the statement is not true, write *False.*

1. Sales slips help to keep inventory records up to date.

2. It is important to make sure that the information on a sales slip is correct because it is against the law to make a mistake on one.

3. An order letter is a good record of exactly what was ordered and when it was ordered.

4. Sometimes merchandise is ordered by phone.

5. A follow-up letter has some of the same information in it that an order letter includes.

6. An incomplete sales slip may cause problems with keeping an accurate inventory.

7. In a follow-up letter, the writer must carefully describe the problem and explain how it should be corrected.

8. If sales slips are not figured correctly, only the customer can get cheated.

CHAPTER 11

Communicating
With the Public

Henry Fairchild works as a clerk in an office. One of his most important duties is talking with his company's customers and writing to them. He answers nearly all the telephone calls that come to his company. He sees that customers get their questions answered and that they get to talk to the right people. He also answers all letters that request general information from his company.

Henry works for Smith, Haley, and Frank, which is an insurance company. Mr. Smith says that Henry's job is most important because he is often the first person to talk to or correspond with new customers. Mr. Smith feels that whether or not Henry makes a good impression can make all the difference between getting a new customer or not.

Therefore, supervisors in the company were very careful when they promoted Henry to this job. They wanted to get the best possible person. They wanted someone who was a good communicator—someone who did a good job talking to or writing to customers.

His supervisors have been so pleased with the job that Henry is doing that they have now asked him to train someone to help him. Their company is growing fast, and the job has become too big for one person. They want Henry to supervise this new person.

Mildred Keyes has been hired for Henry to train. She speaks politely, uses English well, and has a pleasant personality. Smith, Haley, and Frank think that Henry can teach Mildred how to do the rest of the job.

Lesson 1: Practicing Telephone Manners

The first thing that Henry felt Mildred should know about was good manners when answering the telephone. He told her that her voice and manner would be the first impression many people had of their company. The company wanted that impression to be a good one.

"An unpleasant *tone* in your voice can make customers decide that they will buy their insurance from someone else," explained Henry. "It is a good idea to imagine a person's face when you answer the phone. You want to make that face smile. You want that person to feel comfortable and to know that we want his or her business."

On pages 181 and 182 are eight tips that Henry gave Mildred about telephone manners.

1. Pick up the phone after the first or second ring. It is not a good idea to let the phone ring longer than that. Being slow to answer the phone makes the customer feel that you don't care.

2. Make your voice pleasant but not insincere.

3. Identify the name of the company and then give your name. You would say, "Smith, Haley, and Frank Insurance Company. Mildred Keys speaking."

4. Listen very carefully. Nothing is more annoying to a customer than being asked to repeat what he or she said because you weren't listening.

5. Always be polite, friendly, and helpful. Even if the customer is unpleasant, keep your friendly, cooperative manner. Never get nasty or rude.

6. If you must take a message, make sure that it is accurate and complete. Be sure that the message gets to the person for whom it was intended.

7. End the call by making the customer feel that you care about what was said, that you will do everything necessary to take care of his or her problem, and that you were glad to be able to help.

8. Let the customer hang up first. That way you are certain that the customer has said everything he or she wants to say.

Mildred studied carefully the eight hints that Henry gave her. She was surprised that some of these hints about telephone manners were new to her.

Henry told Mildred that she would have to practice using these tips. The more she practiced, the better she would be at answering the telephone. Mildred wanted to improve her telephone manners. She understood that good telephone manners were important to her company. She wanted to make a good impression every time she talked to customers on the telephone.

Activity A: Number your paper from 1 to 11. Read the hints for good telephone manners listed below. Decide what word or words are missing from each sentence. On your own paper, write the word or words that correctly complete each sentence.

1. Pick up the telephone on the _____ or _____ ring.
2. If you let the phone ring too long, it makes the customer feel that you don't _____ .
3. Make your voice _____ but not _____ .
4. Give the _____ of your company when you answer the telephone.
5. Then give your _____ .
6. Listen _____ .
7. Don't make the customer _____ what he or she has already said.
8. Be polite, _____ , and _____ .
9. If the customer is _____ , don't get _____ .
10. Sometimes you will have to take a _____ .
11. Make sure that it is _____ and _____ .

Activity B: Listed below are some remarks that customers on the telephone might make to you. On a separate sheet of paper, write down what you would say in response.

1. "What company did you say this was?"
2. "What do you mean that Mr. Jones is not available? Stop trying to give me the run-around."
3. "You make sure that Mr. Jones gets my message."
4. "My name is Mr. Kzidklsl." (The voice is unclear. You cannot understand what the person has said.)
5. "Have Mr. Jones call me at 555-9846 before three o'clock."

Activity C: Listed below are the eight tips that Henry gave Mildred about telephone manners. However, the hints are out of order. On your own paper, number from 1 to 8. Write the letters of these hints in the order in which they should be done.

a. End the call by making the customer feel that you care about what was said and that you were glad to help.
b. Make your voice pleasant but not insincere.
c. Be polite, friendly, and helpful. Even if the customer is unpleasant, keep your friendly manner.
d. Pick up the phone after the first or second ring.
e. If you must take a message, make sure that it is accurate and complete.
f. Listen carefully.
g. Let the customer hang up first.
h. Identify the name of the company and then give your name.

Taking Care of the Customer

"These hints are not all there is to talking to people on the telephone, Mildred," warned Henry. "Once customers tell why they are calling, you have to know what to do."

"What do you mean?" asked Mildred.

"Well," said Henry. "Let's take things one step at a time. Suppose the customer asks to speak to Mr. Smith. There are several possibilities you have to think about. If Mr. Smith is in and taking calls, you can say, 'One minute, please; I'll connect you with Mr. Smith.' If you buzz him, and he's not in his office, what would you do next?"

"I would call him on the office *intercom*. If he doesn't answer, I would tell the customer that I cannot reach him and offer to take a message," explained Mildred.

"Good, Mildred," exclaimed Henry. "However, always remember that if you have to keep a customer waiting on the line more than ten or fifteen seconds, you should get back to the customer and explain why. Now, suppose when the customer calls, he doesn't give his name. How do you ask for it?"

"I guess I could say, 'May I have your name, please?' " replied Mildred.

"Yes, you could. A better question to ask is, 'May I tell Mr. Smith who is calling?' " said Henry. "If Mr. Smith isn't in or can't be reached, here are some other things you can do."

1. You can ask if anyone else can help the customer.
2. You can offer to help.
3. You can offer to take a message for Mr. Smith.
4. You can offer to have Mr. Smith call the customer back.

Activity D: On a separate sheet of paper, write the answers to these questions.

1. Why is it important not to keep customers waiting on the telephone for more than ten or fifteen seconds?
2. If the person the customer wants to talk to is not available, what four things can be done?
3. Why is the person who answers the telephone so important to a company?

Activity E: Listed below are some situations that you might run into when answering a business telephone. On your own paper, write how you would handle each situation. Remember that you want to make the customer happy.

Situation 1:   The customer asks to speak to Mr. Haley. Mr. Haley is out of town at a business meeting.

Situation 2:   The customer asks to speak to Mr. Fine. Mr. Fine is out to lunch now. However, he will be back in the office at 1:30 p.m.

Situation 3:   The customer is thinking about increasing his life insurance. He wants to talk to somebody who can give him advice. Mr. Smith is the company expert on life insurance.

Situation 4:   The customer just got the bill for his insurance premium. He thinks that his bill is too high. He is very angry. Your billing department handles sending out bills.

Situation 5:   Mr. Haley is the company expert on automobile insurance. He is out of town. Mr. Fine also knows about automobile insurance. The customer on the telephone wants to talk to someone about switching his automobile insurance coverage from his present company to your company.

Situation 6:   You have been told that John Acree is a very important customer. He calls and wants to speak to anybody available.

Lesson 2: Taking a Message and Transferring Calls

When they are speaking to customers, it is important for employees to take *messages* and to transfer calls correctly. First, let's consider taking messages. Henry knew that one of the most important steps in answering telephone calls was being able to take accurate, clear, and complete messages. He gave Mildred the following suggestions.

1. Keep a pad of message forms, a pen, and a pencil near your phone at all times.

2. Find out the person to whom the customer wants to speak. Write that person's name on the correct line of the message form.

3. Fill in the date and the time accurately. If the call is made at 9 a.m., make sure you write "a.m."

4. Then write the name of the person who called, what company he or she is with, and the caller's phone number and *extension*. If it is a long distance call, get the *area code* to identify the proper telephone service area.

5. Then check the appropriate box or boxes on the message form (Telephoned, Called to see you, Wants to see you, Please call, Will call again, Urgent, or Returned your call).

6. Write any additional message the caller may have given.

7. Finally, sign your name at the bottom of the form. Then the person receiving the message will know who took it and can ask any questions he or she may have about this message.

You must be correct when you take a message. If you are not sure how to spell the caller's name, ask. If you had trouble hearing some information the caller gave you, ask the caller to repeat it. It is a good idea to repeat the message to the caller to make sure you got it right.

Below is a sample form Henry gave Mildred. Study it carefully.

To: *K. Smith*	
Date: *9 / 5 / 97*	Time: *10:15 a.m.*

WHILE YOU WERE OUT

M *rs. Mary Tyler*
of *Tyler Associates*
Phone: ———   *555-1700*   *36*
           Area Code   Number   Extension

TELEPHONED	√	PLEASE CALL	√
CALLED TO SEE YOU		WILL CALL AGAIN	
WANTS TO SEE YOU		URGENT	
RETURNED YOUR CALL			

Message: *She needs an explanation regarding the insurance on her office.*

Call taken by: *Henry Fairchild*

Notice that the person writing on the message form filled in every bit of information necessary for the person receiving the message. Remember that clear handwriting is important. The person who reads the message will need to make out the spelling of each name. The person who took this message also wrote the numbers with great care. Correct numbers are especially important. When some numbers are not written clearly, they can be mistaken for other numbers. The person receiving the message might not be sure if one number is a 6 or a 0, a 1 or a 7, or a 3 or a 5.

The person who took the message was careful to check the appropriate boxes in the middle of the form. Mr. Smith knows that he is to call Mary Tyler back. Mr. Smith also knows who took the message because Henry signed his full name at the bottom of the form.

Activity A: Shown below is a message form that has not been filled out correctly. On a separate sheet of paper, list the eight mistakes on this message form.

To: *Joe*	
Date:	Time: *9:38*

WHILE YOU WERE OUT

M *Eagles*

of

Phone: _____ *555-9876* _____

| Area Code | Number | Extension |

TELEPHONED		PLEASE CALL	
CALLED TO SEE YOU		WILL CALL AGAIN	
WANTS TO SEE YOU		URGENT	
	RETURNED YOUR CALL		

Message: *wants an estimate on homeowners insurance*

Call taken by: _____

Activity B: Read the following statements. On your own paper, number from 1 to 5. Then write *True* or *False* for each statement below.

1. The only thing you have to keep by your phone to take messages is a pencil.

2. It is not important to find out the name of the caller.

3. Write all numbers carefully so that they can be read.

4. You don't have to bother checking a box on the message form.

5. The person getting the message doesn't have to know who took the message.

Transferring Calls

Transferring business calls correctly is as important as taking accurate messages. Sometimes it is necessary for Henry and Mildred to transfer telephone calls that come in to Smith, Haley, and Frank. If Henry or Mildred cannot help the person who is calling, they must *transfer* or switch that call to another department or to another person in the company.

Henry told Mildred that when she has to transfer a call, she should first explain to the caller why she must transfer him or her to someone else.

Next, Mildred must be sure to give the caller the name and extension number to which the call is being transferred. Then, if the caller accidentally gets *disconnected,* he or she can call back and ask for the right person.

Then Henry showed Mildred how to transfer a customer's call on their business phone. Mildred has to make sure that she uses the correct method for transferring a customer's call so that she does nothing to disconnect the caller. Finally, Henry told her to stay on the line until she is sure that the caller has been transferred to the correct party or office.

Henry explained to Mildred that more people hang up when calls are being transferred than at any other time. Transfers must be made quickly so that the customer does not get tired of holding the telephone and hang up.

Activity C: Listed below are the steps that you should follow when transferring a call, but they are not in the right order. On a separate piece of paper, number from 1 to 4. Write the letters of the steps in the right order. Begin with the step that you should do first.

a. Use the correct method for transferring a call.

b. Explain why you have to transfer this call.

c. Stay with the caller until he or she has been transferred to the right person or department.

d. Give the caller the name and extension of the person to whom you are transferring the call.

Lesson 3: Taking Minutes of Meetings

Henry told Mildred that there was another part of their job that they had not discussed yet. Every once in a while, one of the bosses would ask either Henry or Mildred to sit in on a business meeting and take minutes.

Minutes are an official written record of what happens at a meeting. Such notes are important because they are filed as an official record of what took place at the meeting. Therefore, the person who takes the minutes has a big responsibility. He or she must take careful, accurate notes. The minutes must be a record of what actually happened, with no interpretation of those events by the person who is taking the minutes.

Mildred had never taken minutes before. She was worried about this part of the job, so she asked Henry to give her some tips on how to take minutes.

Henry gave Mildred this list of suggestions on how to take minutes at a meeting.

1. Take notes on anything that happens that you think is important. You can summarize discussion, but you must take down word for word any motions or resolutions that are made. A *motion* is a formal call for action or a proposal made at a meeting. For example, someone might say, "I make a motion that we spend $10,000 for advertising." A *resolution* is a formal statement of a decision or an expression of opinion voted by an official body or assembled group. Include the names of the people who make the motions or resolutions and the names of the people who second them. To *second* means to state that one agrees with or supports a motion under discussion.

2. If you do not understand something that is being discussed, ask about it during the meeting.

3. Type your final minutes as soon after the meeting as possible. Then what happened at the meeting will be fresh in your mind.

4. Remember that the minutes you write must be accurate and *objective*. Deal only with facts. Do not let personal feelings, prejudices, or interpretations influence your notes. Your minutes must summarize the decisions made and the actions taken at the meeting.

Henry also explained that Mildred would be given an agenda when she got to the meeting. An *agenda* is a list of topics that are going to be discussed at the meeting. The list is in the order in which each topic will be discussed. The agenda will help you to follow the meeting and to organize your notes.

Note Taking

"Write down key words and phrases that will help you to remember what was discussed," Henry told Mildred. "In most cases, don't try to write down every word. Summarize general discussion and debated ideas. Abbreviate words, if you wish. For example, suppose a committee is talking about ways to get more customers. Mr. Frank suggests that the company advertise in the newspaper. You might write down something that looks like this."

Frank — adv. in paper

"If Mr. Haley suggests advertising in all the media, you might write down something that looks like this."

Haley — adv. in all media

"Formal suggestions like motions or resolutions must be taken down word for word. Use quotation marks. Names and figures must be written exactly. For example, if Mr. Smith makes a motion that they budget $100,000 for advertising in all media and Mr. Fairly seconds it, you might write down something that looks like this."

Smith – "I move that we budget $10,000 for advertising in all media."
Fairly – seconded

"Remember," warned Henry. "Everybody takes notes differently. Write down what you need to remember about what happened at the meeting. Later, you will use those notes to write good, complete sentences and paragraphs that other people can read and understand."

"Writing minutes is a hard job," said Henry. "It takes a lot of practice. The more you do it, the easier it will become and the better you will do it. The big secret is to listen carefully and to take accurate notes."

Activity A: Given below is a part of a discussion from a meeting. On a separate sheet of paper, write the notes you would take from this discussion.

Ms. Ives: Because of all the problems we have had with collecting premiums from some of our customers, I move that we hire a collection agency to collect any bill that is over ninety days past due.

Mr. King: Before we vote on that motion, I believe we should look into how much a collection agency will cost us. Also there should be some things the billing department can do before we get outside help.

Mr. Rodgers: You're right. I think the billing department could make more calls to customers with overdue bills—maybe even send them one or two warning letters.

Ms. Ives: I agree that we should look into that aspect of it. Let's have Ms. Raye, who is in charge of the billing department, come to our next meeting to report on what her department is doing and what more they can do.

Ms. Charles: Would you put that in the form of motion, please, Ms. Ives?

Ms. Ives: I move that we table my original motion and that we have Ms. Raye report at our next meeting on what the billing department is doing and can do to collect delinquent accounts.

Mr. Rodgers: I second that motion.

Ms. Charles: All in favor? Then the motion is carried.

Activity B: Use the notes you took in Activity A and write minutes for that part of the meeting. Try not to refer back to the actual discussion in the textbook. Use only your notes to write your minutes on a separate sheet of paper.

Lesson 4: Giving Information in Letters

Sometimes Smith, Haley, and Frank deal with customers who live out of town. These customers sometimes call long distance or write letters with questions that they need to have answered.

Part of Henry and Mildred's jobs is to answer requests for general information. For example, a customer who lives in Philadelphia called. That customer wanted to know if his homeowners insurance covered the theft of his lawn chairs from his front lawn. Henry said that he would check the insurance coverage and write the customer a letter.

Shown below is part of the body of the letter that Henry wrote to this customer in Philadelphia.

You have our standard homeowners policy. This policy covers you for all loss by theft after the first $100. Since your policy has a $100 *deductible* clause, you must pay the first $100 of loss, and we will pay any loss over $100. If the value of your lawn chairs comes to more than $100, send us the receipt for the cost of the replacements. We will send you a check for any amount over $100.

Henry's letter is a very good one. He states the kind of policy this customer has and describes the coverage. He explains how much the customer will have to pay to replace his lawn chairs and how much the insurance company will pay. He tells the customer exactly what to do.

Activity A: Shown below is part of a letter written to another customer. This customer wanted to know how he could increase his life insurance coverage. Look at the answer he received. On a separate sheet of paper, write down what should have been included in the answer but wasn't. Then rewrite the body of the letter to make it better.

According to our records, you presently hold $50,000 worth of life insurance. You can increase that amount of insurance if you wish. I would certainly recommend that you double your present coverage, especially in light of the fact that you are married and have two small children.

If I can be of any further assistance, please call me.

Activity B: Write *True* or *False* for each statement.

1. When responding to a letter in which a customer has asked a question, it is important to give the customer all the facts that will clarify and completely answer his or her question.
2. A letter answering a question should be as short as possible.
3. Make a customer feel that you take his or her question seriously and answer it carefully.
4. It is a good idea to provide every bit of information you can when answering a question from a customer.

Activity C: Suppose Mrs. Irene Smith has written you a letter asking what kinds of transportation are used in your city or town. Are there buses or taxicabs that she can take? Is there a subway? Is there a place where she can rent a car or hire a driver? On a separate sheet of paper, write a letter to Mrs. Smith. Give as much information as you can about the transportation available where you live.

Hint: Answer all of Mrs. Smith's questions.   Do not supply any information for which she has not asked. Make sure that what you have written is clear, easy to understand, accurate, and complete.

Summary

Being able to communicate with other people is very important to both Henry and Mildred on their job. If you stop and think about it, you will realize that, no matter what your job is, you will have to be able to speak and to write clearly. Every job requires that you make yourself understood.

Misunderstandings on the job can create expensive mistakes. These mistakes can cost a company or customers much money. Misunderstandings on the job can also cause serious accidents. Misunderstandings on the job can waste time and can delay a job or project from being completed on time.

It is easy to understand why employers want good communicators working for them. They don't have the time or money to spend on people who can't say or write what they mean.

Remember these nine important points about communicating on the job.

1. Always be polite and try to be helpful.

2. Listen carefully to what is being said to you.

3. If you are not sure you understood something, ask for an explanation.

4. If you don't know how to spell a person's name, ask how to spell it.

5. Always have a friendly tone to your voice.

6. Make the customer feel that you really care about him or her.

7. Make everything you write complete, clear, easy to read, and accurate.

8. Use neat, careful handwriting.

9. When questions are asked, try to answer them. If you cannot answer the questions, take time to find the answer for the customer.   If necessary, transfer the caller to someone else who can help.

CHAPTER REVIEW

Review Activity A: The words in these five statements are scrambled. On your own paper, rewrite each statement correctly.

try be always helpful polite and to
said carefully what to to listen is you being
understand if ask explanation you an something not for do
feel make care her the or about customer you him really that
careful use handwriting neat

Review Activity B: Write *True* or *False* for each statement below.

1. An unpleasant voice answering the telephone can make a customer decide to go elsewhere.
2. When the phone rings, count to ten before you pick up the receiver.
3. If you answer the telephone right away, the customer will think that you are not busy.
4. Make your voice sound pleasant.
5. Give the name of your company.
6. Don't give your name unless the caller asks for it.
7. Do not ask callers to repeat unless you didn't understand them.
8. If the customer gets nasty, you get rude, too.
9. Make sure that any message you take is complete and accurate.
10. End the call quickly. You don't have time to waste on the telephone.
11. Make customers feel you will do everything you can to help them.
12. Do not mumble.
13. It is all right to use slang as long as you are courteous to the caller.
14. Hang up if the customer keeps right on talking.
15. Let customers hang up first. Then you can be sure that they have said everything they want to say.

Review Activity C: Listed below are three situations that you might run into when answering a business telephone. On your own paper, write how you would handle each situation.

Situation 1:   Mrs. Smith, who is a very important customer, has called and wants to speak to your boss. Your boss has told you that if Mrs. Smith should call today, he doesn't have time to talk to her. What do you tell Mrs. Smith?

Situation 2:   Your immediate supervisor has gone out to lunch. Her boss calls and wants to speak with her immediately. What do you do?

Situation 3:   Your boss has left word that he does not wish to take any phone calls for the next hour. What do you do when someone asks to speak to him?

Review Activity D: Read the telephone call given below. On your own paper, write the message you would give to your boss as a result of this phone call.

You: H. G. Thomas Company. Ms. Ward speaking.

Caller: Ms. Ward, this is John Denny. I would like to speak to Mr. Thomas.

You: I'm sorry, Mr. Denny, but Mr. Thomas is in a meeting now. May I take a message?

Caller: Yes, tell him to call me as soon as possible at 555-8746. The order he sent me is missing several items, and I want to know why.

Review Activity E: On a separate sheet of paper, list the four things you should do when transferring a call.

Review Activity F: Read the suggestions for writing minutes below. Decide what words are missing in each case. Use the words listed in the box to help you. On your own paper, write the correct word or words to complete each sentence.

fresh	second	discussed
actions	minutes	resolutions
important	decisions	names
objective	motions	word for word
discussion	possible	accurate

1. Sometimes you will have to take notes for _____ at meetings.
2. Take notes on anything that you think is _____ .
3. Summarize any _____ during the meeting.
4. You must take down _____ any _____ or _____ that are made.
5. Include the _____ of the people who make the motions or resolutions.
6. Also include the names of the people who _____ them.
7. If you do not understand something that is being _____ , ask about it during the meeting.
8. Write up your notes as soon after the meeting as _____ .
9. Then what happened at the meeting will be _____ in your mind.
10. The minutes you write must be _____ and _____ .
11. They must summarize the _____ made and the _____ taken at the meeting.

Review Activity G: Shown below is a part of a discussion from a meeting. On a separate sheet of paper, write the notes you would take from that discussion.

Mr. Smith: I think that we should hire at least three new salespeople. The load is getting very heavy for the salespeople we have now.

Ms. George: Have you talked with our present sales staff? Don't forget, these people work on commission, and they may not want to share customers with new employees. Have they said they feel overworked?

Mr. Smith: Yes, they have. They complain a lot, but I haven't talked to them about whether they would like us to bring in more salespeople.

Mr. Haley: I'm not sure the sales staff should make that decision. Are our customers complaining about the service they're getting?

Ms. George: I haven't gotten any complaints.

Mr. Haley: Then I don't see what the problem is. You know that sales staff always complain. They'll complain no matter what we do.

Mr. Smith: I'd feel happier if I could ask them how they'd feel about our adding to the sales staff.

Ms. George: I move that Mr. Smith poll the sales staff to see if they feel that they need help. If they feel that they are overworked, then we will hire additional salespeople.

Mr. Smith: I second that motion.

Mr. Haley: All in favor? The motion is passed.

Review Activity H: Use the notes you took in Review Activity G and write minutes for that part of the meeting. Use only your notes to write your minutes. Use a separate sheet of paper.

Review Activity I: Suppose that Mr. Howard Fast wrote to your company to ask whether or not it would sell him automobile insurance. The first thing your company would want to do is check Mr. Fast's driving record. If his driving record is poor, your company probably would not want to insure him. If his driving record is good, your company probably would want to insure him. On a separate sheet of paper, write a letter to Mr. Fast. In the letter, tell whether or not your company will sell him automobile insurance and why. You decide whether or not he has a good driving record.

Review Activity J: Suppose that your boss asked you to write a letter to Ms. Carole Dryer. You are going to ask her to complete a form. You are enclosing this form with your letter, and she is to return it within a week's time to your boss. On a separate sheet of paper, write the letter to Ms. Dryer for your boss. Be sure to include everything that he has asked you to include. An enclosure is something that is being sent with a letter, such as a form or a copy of a sales slip or invoice. Will there be an enclosure with this letter? What will it be?

Review Activity K: Look at pages 197 and 198. Study the summary of this chapter carefully. Find the suggestions from the summary that are important for communicating on the job. List these suggestions briefly on a separate sheet of paper.

CHAPTER 12

Getting Ahead

Ralph Baines was concerned about his career at Stick and Stuck Mills. He had worked for the same company for eight years. During the first three years, he was promoted several times. Since then he had not received a single promotion. One night he talked about his situation to Mel Travis, who worked for the same company. Mel had been promoted steadily during the ten years he worked for Stick and Stuck.

Lesson 1: Additional Training

"Mel, why don't I get promoted the way you do?" asked Ralph.

"Because you don't bother getting additional training," replied Mel. "You laugh at me when I go to night school or to the college to take courses, but our company is changing. You have to change, too. My next project is to get training in programming computers."

"What has programming got to do with a fabric mill?" asked Ralph.

"Plenty, and you'd know that if you kept up with what our company is doing. Six months from now the company is installing two looms that work by computer. If those work out, we will install more. What do you think will happen to the men who work the machines now?" Mel asked.

"They'll get laid off. Hey, I work on those machines. Do you think I could be fired or laid off?" Ralph asked in a worried voice.

"Our company doesn't have a retraining program. People have to get their own training. I bet if you can't operate a computer, you'll be out," Mel responded.

"What am I going to do?" wondered Ralph.

"Well, you could join me and take these two courses at the college on computers. The first course is an introduction. The second one covers beginning programming," suggested Mel. "I want to sign up next semester for advanced programming. The courses are given at night. You'd have to go two nights a week."

"Well, that doesn't excite me," said Ralph. "but I'll think about it."

"Don't wait too long, Ralph. You have to register next week," explained Mel. "If we don't enroll in time, we probably won't get into those courses. They're two of the most popular ones the school offers."

Ralph went home and discussed the idea of additional training with his wife. Sara thought that going to school was a good idea. "You've been upset about not getting ahead in the company. If this schooling will help you, I think you should do it," said Sara. "Why don't you talk to your boss and ask him if he thinks it's a good idea?"

The next day Ralph did just what Sara suggested. His boss said, "Ralph, I'm so glad you're thinking about doing something to improve your skills. I was beginning to feel that you didn't want to put forth the effort to do better. Taking these computer courses may be the best decision you ever made. We will need people with that kind of training to serve as supervisors."

The following week Ralph and Mel went to the college to register for the courses they wanted to take. There were lines of people, some signing up to take courses and some to pay for the courses they just enrolled in. There were also forms to fill out. Some of the forms were confusing to Ralph. The forms might confuse you, too. Later in this lesson you will study the vocabulary that appears on some of these forms.

It is helpful to know that people go to school for different reasons. Some, like Ralph, go to take a few courses to improve their job skills or to learn more about a certain subject. Others go to take courses to earn a degree.

Several types of college degrees exist. One degree is called an associate of arts degree. To get this degree, you must complete a program that contains two years' worth of courses. Another kind of degree college students can earn is called an *undergraduate degree.* An undergraduate or bachelor's degree means that you've gone to college long enough and taken enough classes to complete four years' worth of courses in a program offered by the university or college. After earning this undergraduate degree, a person may choose to go on and enroll in a graduate program. Such a person wants to go even further with his or her education. He or she could earn a master's degree or a doctorate.

Listed below are some words that are commonly found on college forms. Read the definitions of these words carefully.

College Form Vocabulary

Course number — a number given to a course to show that it is different from all the other courses. Course numbers are found in college catalogs and course listings.

Course title — the name of the course; for example, "Computers for the Beginner" or "Computers I."

Course description — an explanation of what is taught in a college course. This information is usually found in the catalog.

Degree desired — The degree program that a student is working to complete; examples include A. A., B. A., or B. S. (Associate of Arts, Bachelor of Arts, or Bachelor of Science).

Section — One particular class out of several that may be offered of the same course.

Credit—Points given by a college to a student who has successfully finished a course.

On the next page is an example of the *registration form* that Ralph filled out to sign up for college courses. Study this registration form carefully.

Strasburgh College
Registration Form

(Please print or type.)

Name _____ Baines, _____ Ralph _____ F. _____
              Last   First   Middle Initial

Address _____ 10 Elm Street _____

_____ Miami, _____ Florida _____ 33153 _____
              City   State   ZIP

Course No.	Section	Title	Days Offered	Credits
736 - 1000	3	Computer I	Tu	3
736 - 1004	1	Programming I	W	3

Ralph F. Baines
Signature

Ralph printed his name and address according to the instructions on the form. He checked the college catalog to get the correct course number and title. The section number, days offered, and credits were copied from a course listing given to Ralph when he went to register.

Ralph was very careful in filling out this form. He wanted to make sure that he ended up in the class he wanted to take. He asked Mel to check the form for him to see that he had completed it correctly. Asking Mel to read it was a good way to double-check that everything was right.

Activity A: Number your paper from 1 to 7. Match the college form vocabulary words in the first column with their meanings in the second column. Write the correct letter for each number.

Vocabulary Word	**Meaning**
1. course description	a. Number assigned to a course to tell it from other courses
2. days offered	b. The day or days of the week when you will attend school to take the course
3. section	c. The program taken to earn an associate or bachelor's degree
4. course number	d. The name of the course
5. credit	e. An explanation of what will be taught in the course
6. course title	f. The particular class of a given course
7. degree desired	g. The number of points to be earned for this course

Lesson 2: Other Forms

Ralph's friend, Peg Taylor, is taking courses, too. However, Peg is planning to get her degree from Central College. In addition to the forms that Ralph and Mel filled out, she completed a *college application* for admission to college as a *degree candidate*. That term describes someone trying to complete a degree program and earn a college diploma. The form was five pages long. When Peg showed it to Ralph, he laughed and said, "Just having to fill out all that information would keep me up all night!"

"No, it wouldn't," smiled Peg. "It's not hard to complete these forms once you understand what information they're asking for." Look at the first page of the application that Peg completed. Study it carefully.

Application for CENTRAL COLLEGE

(Miss)
Mrs.

1. Name in full: Mr.   Taylor   Peggy   Marsha   2.   Sex F
                          Last   First   Middle

3. Permanent Home Address ___211 5th Street___ Miami   Dade   FL   33152
                          Number/Route Street   City   County State ZIP

   Mailing address (if different from #3) _____
                          Number/Route Street   City   County State ZIP

4. Soc. Sec. No. 318-58-0745   Phone No. 271-3122   Emergency Phone No. 271-4873

5. (a) Date of birth ___2 / 12 / 68___   Age 31   (b) Place of birth Ocala, FL
                       Month / Day/ Year

   (c) If not born in the United States, when and where were you naturalized?_____

6. Married   Yes _____   No √ _____   1918 Sun Street

7. Name and   Father Samuel Taylor   Ocala, FL 32670   Phone No. 586-1621
   address of   Mother Elaine Taylor   Same   Phone No. Same
                Guardian _____   Phone No. _____

8. (a) List all senior high schools attended:

Name of School	Location	Years of Attendance	Date of Graduation
Ocala Senior High	Ocala, FL	1983 - 1986	1986

   (b) Have you received a GED? Yes ___ No √ Date you received your GED:_____
   I (have taken) I plan to take the Scholastic Aptitude Test (Date) _7 / 6 / 98_ and will have the results forwarded.

9. (a) List all colleges and/or universities attended:

Name	City & State	Dates Attended	Reasons for Leaving	# of Credits Completed
N / A				

   (b) If ever suspended or dismissed, please explain in detail on separate attached sheet.
   (c) Have you ever attended Central College? No   Full ___ Part-Time ___ Evening ___
        Summer _____ Last Date _____

10. (a) In what extracurricular activities have you participated in high school; for example, athletics, dramatics, music, publications, etc. List offices held. List in order of preference.
        1. Newspaper (editor)   2. Yearbook
        3. Glee Club   4. _____

    (b) Name any special honors you have received in school Honor Roll

11. Work experiences, including summer or part-time employment. If you are not a recent high school graduate, you must account for each year intervening between date of leaving high school and date of this application. (Use separate sheet if necessary)

Type of Work	Name and Address of Employer	Phone Number	Dates of Employment	Part- or Full-Time	Salary
Clerk-Typist	S. Franz, 2387 Flagler St. Miami, FL 33154	383-1175	1986 to Present	Full-time	$19,370 per year

Activity A: Now that you have studied Peg's college application, you should have an idea of what information is needed. On a separate sheet of paper, number from 1 to 10. Then match the item from the application in the first column with the information you would need to complete that item in the second column. Write the correct letter next to each number.

Application Item

1. Emergency phone number

2. Place of birth

3. Married

4. List colleges attended

5. Extracurricular activities

6. Work experiences

7. Type of work

8. Dates of employment

9. Salary

10. Years of attendance

Information Needed

a. Date when you began to work for a company and date when you stopped working for that company

b. A number the college can call to inform someone if you are sick or hurt

c. The city and state where you were born

d. A list of the jobs you have held up to this time

e. Are you married? Answer yes or no.

f. Clubs or organizations you joined in school and which were not part of the regular school program

g. The kind of work that you did for a company

h. The amount you were paid

i. The year you started in a school and the year you left that school

j. The names of colleges you attended

Another friend of Ralph's was taking an *adult education* course at the night school being run in a local high school. There are several reasons why people attend this kind of night school. One reason is to take a course to get a special skill, such as tailoring, typing, etc. Another is to learn more about a certain subject. A third reason is to complete high school, because this kind of school offers high school courses at night. People who didn't graduate earlier can go back and earn their high school diploma.

Ralph's friend had not graduated from high school and wanted to finish at night. He asked Ralph for some help in filling out the form for applying for night school.

Grand City Public Schools — Adult Education Division
Night-School Application

(Please print or type.)

Smith	Oscar	T.
Name (Last)	(First)	(Initial)

27 Lynch Circle	33162
Address	(ZIP Code)

444 - 1112	555 - 2899
Telephone Number	Emergency Telephone

Flagler High School,   1700 Rise Drive
Name and Address of Last School Attended

10th	1982
Highest Grade Completed	Last Year Attended

How did you find out about this night-school center?
A neighbor told me.

What are your educational goals?
I would like to get my high school diploma.

List below the course or courses you wish to take.
English III   Algebra I

Activity B: Study the application, shown on page 212, that Ralph's friend filled out. Then, on your own paper, answer these questions about that form.

1. Why do you think the instructions ask that you print or type?

2. What is Mr. Smith's first name and middle initial?

3. What is his ZIP code?

4. If Mr. Smith got sick at school or had an accident, what number should the people in the school call?

5. Where did Mr. Smith go to high school?

6. When did he leave high school?

7. Did he graduate from high school? What evidence is there on the application to prove your answer?

8. How did Mr. Smith find out about this night school?

9. What two courses does Mr. Smith want to take at night school this semester?

10. Do you think this is the only semester he will attend night school? Prove your answer by citing some information on the application.

11. Many night schools have guidance counselors who work with students to make sure that they get the best program. Why do you think the counselor would be especially interested in a person's educational goals?

12. Why do you think the application asks for the name and address of the last school attended?

Lesson 3: Test-Taking Skills

After a few weeks of their course, Mel and Ralph's teacher announced that there would be a test the following week. "I've been dreading that," moaned Ralph. "It's been years since I took a test, and I did not always do very well then. Sometimes I get so nervous that I can't think straight."

"Do you think you understand everything we've learned in class?" asked Mel.

"Yes, I do. In fact, I feel very sure of what we have learned. I've studied between classes, read all the chapters the teacher assigned, and did all the homework. Tests just bother me."

"They used to bother me, but in one of my courses, the teacher took time to teach some techniques for handling tests. I haven't had any trouble since," said Mel.

"Tell me about some good techniques, Mel. You just might help me get a great grade!"

These are the techniques that Mel explained to Ralph.

1. Make sure that you know the material thoroughly on which you are being tested.

    Do not wait until just before a test to study. Study each new piece of material as it is given to you. Keep up with reading assignments. Take careful notes as you read. Review each set of notes regularly. If things are not clear to you, ask questions in class.

2. Budget the time that you have to take the test.

   Before you begin the test, look it over. Count the number and type of questions. Figure out how much time you have for the whole test and how much time you can devote to each question. True/false and multiple-choice questions usually require the least amount of time. Questions that require a two- or three-sentence response require more time. Questions that require an essay-type response require the most time. If you have an hour to complete the test, you should be halfway through in 30 minutes. Pace yourself. If you finish the test early, look over your answers.

3. Read each question carefully.

   Answer the question that is asked, not the question you thought would be asked. Reading a question incorrectly will cause you to give the wrong answer. For example, suppose one question asks, "Where is the input button?" You read quickly and think it says, "When is the input button used?" You certainly would answer the question wrong unless you reread it correctly.

4. Save the questions that you are not sure of for last.

   If you are not sure of an answer, continue with the rest of the test. After you have finished the rest of the test, try to answer any questions that you skipped earlier. If this is the kind of test that has no penalty for unanswered questions, answer only those questions for which you are reasonably sure of the correct response.

5. Concentrate on the parts of the test that are worth the most points.

   If you have been told that some parts of the test are worth more points than others, concentrate on the parts that are worth the most points.

6. If the test you are taking requires using a *preprinted answer sheet,* mark answers clearly and accurately.

   Check the numbering of your own answer sheet often as you place answers on it. Make sure that your markings are dark. If you skip a question, make sure to skip an answer on the answer sheet, too. Go back to skipped questions and answers later.

7. Change answers only if you have a good reason for doing so.

   It is usually best not to change an answer based on a hunch or whim. However, if you believe you have good evidence that your first answer was wrong, change your answer.

Activity A: On your own paper, number from 1 to 16. Read the statements on pages 216 and 217. Write *True* or *False* for each statement.

1. You will do better on a test if you wait to study until right before the test is given.
2. Study each new piece of material as it is given.
3. Do your reading assignments all at one time.
4. Don't ask questions in class; asking questions will make the teacher think that you are dumb.
5. Reading a question incorrectly can cause you to give the wrong answer.
6. Before you begin a test, it is a good idea to look it over first to see how many and what kind of questions the test contains.
7. If you are not sure of the answer to a question, skip it and go on. Come back to the questions you skipped after you finish the rest of the test.
8. Allow the most time for multiple-choice questions and the least time for essay-type questions.

9. If you have been told how much each part of the test is worth, concentrate on those parts that are worth the most points.
10. If you are using a preprinted answer sheet, check the numbering of your answers often.
11. If this is the kind of test where you don't lose points for unanswered questions, guess as many answers as you can.
12. When you do your reading assignments, take careful notes.
13. If you have a hunch that the answer you have given is wrong, it is a good idea to change it.
14. Change an answer only if you are very sure that you are changing to the correct answer.
15. Never skip a question.
16. If you finish the test early, look over your answers.

Activity B: On your own paper, write the answers to these problems.

1. Your test has 20 multiple-choice questions. You have 50 minutes to take the test. About how long should you allow for each question?

2. The true/false section of a test is worth 25 points. The essay section is worth 45. The short-answer section is worth 30. To which part should you devote the most time?

3. You have three hours in which to take a test. It has three parts. The first part has 25 multiple-choice questions. The reading part of each question is fairly long. This part of the test is worth 35 points.
The second part of the test consists of ten questions for which you have to write two- or three-sentence answers. It is worth 20 points.
The last part of the test consists of two essay-type questions. Each question requires an answer that is several paragraphs long. It is worth 45 points.
How will you budget the three hours you have to take this test?

4. You have been given a standardized test that contains 100 multiple-choice questions. You have three hours to take this test. You want to:
   - Answer as many questions as you can.
   - Allow time to check the numbering of your preprinted answer sheet as you work.
   - Go back and try to answer any questions that you skipped.
   - Reread any answers of which you weren't sure.

   How would you budget the three hours you are allowed for this test?

Summary

Sometimes the jobs that you are hired to do change. Every day there are new inventions and ideas that change the way things are done. It is very likely that sometime during your career you will need to be trained to do something different. Often this training means taking courses in colleges, universities, or other adult education centers.

In order to be allowed to enter these programs, you will need to fill out some kind of form. This completed form must be correct and neat.

When you take courses, you will have to take tests. The following suggestions will help you to take these tests: studying the course material, budgeting the time you have to take the test, and reading the questions carefully. It will also help if you spend the most time on the parts of the tests that are worth the most points, mark your answers carefully on preprinted answer sheets, and change your answers only if you have a good reason.

CHAPTER REVIEW

Review Activity A: On a separate sheet of paper, number from 1 to 6. Read the following sentences. Choose the correct word to complete each sentence. Write the correct word or words from the box next to each number on your paper.

course number	days offered
course title	degree desired
credits	description
section	

1. Colleges identify courses in different ways. They always give each course offered a number, which is called the _____ _____ .

2. The catalog also has a _____ of the course to explain what will be taught.

3. However, the surest way to identify a particular class is through the _____ _____ and the _____ number. The course number is assigned to distinguish one course from another. The section number is assigned to distinguish one class of that course from another.

4. You must also know the _____ _____ in order to make sure that you get to the class when you should and to make sure that it fits into your schedule.

5.   The college gives _____ for each course taken. They can be used toward getting a diploma.

6. If you want a diploma, you should indicate the "_____ _____" on your application to take courses.

Review Activity B: Study the registration form below. Find the five errors on this form. List those errors on a separate sheet of paper.

Cross College
Registration Form

(Please print or type.)

Name _____ Bill   W.   Jones _____

            Last   First   Middle Initial

Address _____ 1736 Cove Road _____

        Saginaw   Michigan   48605

         City   State   ZIP

Course No.	Section	Title	Days Offered	Credits
46 - 2911	1		Tu	3
	2	Chemistry I	W	3

_____ *Jones* _____

             Signature

Review Activity C: Listed on pages 220 and 221 are some terms from a college application. On your own paper, write the information that you would place on the lines containing these terms.

1. Emergency Phone No.
2. Date of Birth
3. Place of Birth
4. Name of Father

5. Senior High Attended
6. Date of Graduation
7. Colleges Attended
8. Extracurricular Activities
9. Community Activities
10. Work Experiences

11. Dates of Employment
12. Salary
13. Married
14. Age
15. Years of Attendance
16. Special Honors

Review Activity D: Shown below is a night-school application that was filled out incorrectly.   On another piece of paper, list the ten mistakes on this application.

Grand City Public Schools — Adult Education Division
Night-School Application

(Please print or type.)
        Mary Jane Crawford
_____
Name   (Last)   (First)   (Initial)

 119 8th Street
_____
Address   (ZIP Code)

 555-1122
_____
Telephone Number   Emergency Telephone

 Southside
_____
Name and Address of Last School Attended

    10th
_____
Highest Grade Completed   Last Year Attended

How did you find out about this night-school center?
 I drove around until I got a parking space.
_____

What are your educational goals?
 I want to get a new job.
_____

List below the course or courses you wish to take.
 American History
_____

Review Activity E: Read the following sentences. On your own paper, write the missing words needed to complete each sentence.

1. Make sure that you _____ the directions for a test.
2. If you don't, _____ the teacher to explain the directions.
3. Read the questions _____ .
4. Before you _____ a test, look it over.
5. Count the_____ of questions.
6. Also notice the _____ of questions.
7. Figure out how much time you have for the _____ test.
8. Figure out how much time you can devote to each _____ .
9. Allow the _____ time for true/false questions.
10. Allow the _____ time for essay questions.
11. Spend the most time on the parts of the test that are _____ the most points.

Review Activity F: Listed below are the seven techniques for taking a test that Mel explained to Ralph. However, the words are scrambled. On your own paper, write each of these techniques correctly.

1. that the are on sure material you you make know being tested thoroughly which
2. time have the take you the to budget test that
3. question each read carefully
4. questions you the not of last for are save sure that
5. that points parts concentrate most on worth the of the the test are
6. you requires sheet and are mark using a answers the preprinted test if taking answer accurately clearly
7. if for so answers reason doing change a only you have good

CHAPTER 13

Meeting Emergencies
in Your Job

When Jane Michaels first came to work for Ted E. Baer, Inc., she applied for *medical insurance.* It can help people to pay bills caused by illness, injury, or accident. The *premium,* or payment, for that insurance protection was subtracted from her weekly paycheck. Jane needed health insurance. By getting it through her job, her rates were much lower than if she were to buy it as an individual. Medical insurance is less expensive when a large group of people get it together as *group insurance.* Some companies also offer life insurance in a group plan.

Jane paid for her medical insurance for three years without ever using it. Then she discovered she needed an operation to correct a problem she was having with the ligaments in her wrist. She would be in the hospital two days. Because of her insurance, Jane wouldn't have to pay anything to the hospital or her doctor. Her insurance covered all medical expenses. Jane was very glad that she had medical insurance.

Lesson 1: Getting Health Insurance

Let's go back to those first days that Jane worked for Ted E. Baer, Inc. Jane had to fill out an application in order to get her medical insurance. If she had filled out that application incorrectly, she might not have been able to collect the insurance when she needed it. Shown below is the form that Jane filled in.

Medical Insurance Application

	Michaels	Jane	Janet	Ted E. Baer, Inc.
Name	(Last)	(First)	(Middle)	Employer

1223 Long Blvd. Atlanta, Georgia 98716
Home Address (include ZIP code)

_3 / 12 / 72_   _7 / 21 / 72_
Date of Birth   Spouse's Date of Birth

			No	Does your spouse have
___	Male	___ Single		group health insurance
√	Female	√ Married		with another employer,
0	No. of	___ Widowed		union, etc.?
	dependents	___ Divorced		

Signature _Jane J. Michaels_   Date _3 / 18 / 95_

Notice that Jane followed all the directions carefully. She gave her birth date and the birth date of her husband. She has no children or anyone else who depends on her for their food, shelter, and clothing. Therefore, she has no dependents.

If she had not filled the form out carefully, Jane might have gotten health insurance, but her husband might not have been able to use it. Because her husband is not covered by any other health plan, he will be covered under Jane's. The policies of many health insurance companies work this way.

Activity A: Shown below is a form like the one Jane filled out. Each blank line has a number. On a separate sheet of paper, number from 1 to 11. Then write the information you would write on each line if you were filling out the form for yourself.

Medical Insurance Application

①_____   ②_____
Name   (Last)   (First)   (Middle)   Employer

③_____
Home Address (include ZIP code)

④_____   ⑤_____
Date of Birth   Spouse's Date of Birth

⑥____ Male   ⑦____ Single   ⑧____ Does your spouse have
       Female   ____ Married   group health insurance
⑨____ No. of   ____ Widowed   with another employer,
       dependents   ____ Divorced   union, etc.?

Signature ⑩_____   Date ⑪_____

Lesson 2: Health Insurance Benefits and Forms

When Jane was receiving treatment for medical problems with her wrist, she had to complete more forms. These forms made sure that her health insurance paid her doctor and hospital. Some health insurance is paid directly to the patient; then the patient pays the hospital and doctor. However, Jane's insurance didn't work that way. She filled in forms in order to get the money sent to her doctor by the insurance company. The doctor had to fill out part of the form, too. Jane filled out her part. Then she took the form to her doctor's office so that his secretary could fill in the rest and send it to the insurance company. Sometimes the doctor's office has forms on which you can fill out your part. Then the doctor's office sends them to the insurance company.

Before Jane could fill out her portion of the form, she had to make sure she understood the vocabulary used on the form. She called her insurance company and was given the following information about terms used on this form.

1. *Patient* — The name of the person who is being treated. In Jane's case, she would write her own name. If her husband was the one having the operation, she would write his name on the form.

2. *Employee* or *Insuree* — The name of the employed person who has the insurance. Jane would write her name here, no matter who was being treated. Some forms use the term "insuree's name." It means the same as "employee's name."

3. Do you have other health insurance coverage? — This question asks if you have any other medical insurance and, if you do, the name of the company. In Jane's case, she would write "No." It is important to complete this item carefully. If you say you have other coverage and you don't, your health insurance company may not pay all the benefits to which you are entitled.

4. Was condition related to patient's employment? — This question asks if the medical illness or injury had anything to do with the patient's job. In Jane's case, she would say "No." Her medical problem with her wrist was not caused by her job. This answer also affects the amount of medical benefits paid by the insurance company.

Jane was smart. She called her insurance company for an explanation of insurance terms. That way she was certain of getting the correct answers. After Jane understood these insurance terms, she was able to fill out the form.

Activity A: Listed below are the four terms that Jane asked her insurance company to explain. Beneath each term is its definition. However, some words are missing from the definitions. On your own paper, write the definitions. Complete each sentence with the correct words.

1. Patient's name
   The name of the _____ who is being _____ .

2. Employee's name
   The name of the _____ who carries the _____ .

3. Other insurance coverage
   The name of any other _____ with which you have _____ .

4. Was condition related to patient's employment?
   Did your _____ have anything to do with your job?

Reading a Health Benefit Form

On the next page is a sample of the health benefit form that Jane had to complete so that her doctor and hospital bills could be paid. Study this form carefully. Notice that Jane should not fill out the whole form. The doctor or the person or company supplying the medical service has to complete most of the form.

Remember, if this health benefit form is not filled out correctly, Jane's doctor will not be paid by the insurance company. Jane must be very careful when she completes this form.

MAJOR MEDICAL CLAIM

PATIENT & EMPLOYEE INFORMATION

1 PATIENT'S NAME *(First name, middle initial, last name)*	2 PATIENT'S DATE OF BIRTH	3 EMPLOYEE'S NAME *(First name, middle initial, last name)*
4 PATIENT'S ADDRESS *(Street, city, state, ZIP code)*	5 PATIENT'S SEX MALE FEMALE	6 EMPLOYEE'S DATE OF BIRTH
	7 PATIENT'S RELATIONSHIP TO EMPLOYEE SELF SPOUSE CHILD OTHER	8 EMPLOYEE'S GROUP NO *(Or Group Name)*
9 OTHER HEALTH INSURANCE COVERAGE — Enter Name of Policyholder and Plan Name and Address and Policy or Medical Assistance Number	10 WAS CONDITION RELATED TO A PATIENT'S EMPLOYMENT YES NO B AN AUTO ACCIDENT YES NO	11 EMPLOYEE'S ADDRESS *(Street, city, state, ZIP code)*
12 PATIENT'S OR AUTHORIZED PERSON'S SIGNATURE *I Authorize the Release of any Medical Information Necessary to Process this Claim and Request Payment of MEDICARE CHAMPUS Benefits Either to Myself or to the Party Who Accepts Assignment Below* SIGNED DATE		13 I AUTHORIZE PAYMENT OF MEDICAL BENEFITS TO UNDERSIGNED PHYSICIAN OR SUPPLIER FOR SERVICE DESCRIBED BELOW SIGNED *(Employee or Authorized Person)*

PHYSICIAN OR SUPPLIER INFORMATION

14 DATE OF ILLNESS (FIRST SYMPTOM) OR INJURY (ACCIDENT) OR PREGNANCY (LMP)	15 DATE FIRST CONSULTED YOU FOR THIS CONDITION	16 HAS PATIENT EVER HAD SAME OR SIMILAR SYMPTOMS? YES NO
17 DATE PATIENT ABLE TO RETURN TO WORK	18 DATES OF TOTAL DISABILITY FROM THROUGH	DATES OF PARTIAL DISABILITY FROM THROUGH
19 NAME OF REFERRING PHYSICIAN		20 FOR SERVICES RELATED TO HOSPITALIZATION GIVE HOSPITALIZATION DATES ADMITTED DISCHARGED
21 NAME & ADDRESS OF FACILITY WHERE SERVICES RENDERED *(If other than home or office)*		22 WAS LABORATORY WORK PERFORMED OUTSIDE YOUR OFFICE? YES NO CHARGES

23 DIAGNOSIS OR NATURE OF ILLNESS OR INJURY. RELATE DIAGNOSIS TO PROCEDURE IN COLUMN D BY REFERENCE TO NUMBERS 1, 2, 3, ETC. OR DX CODE

1

2

3

4

24 A DATE OF SERVICE	B PLACE OF SERVICE	C	FULLY DESCRIBE PROCEDURES, MEDICAL SERVICES OR SUPPLIES FURNISHED FOR EACH DATE GIVEN PROCEDURE CODE (IDENTIFY) *(EXPLAIN UNUSUAL SERVICES OR CIRCUMSTANCES)*	D DIAGNOSIS CODE	E CHARGES	F

25 SIGNATURE OF PHYSICIAN OR SUPPLIER	26 ACCEPT ASSIGNMENT *(GOVERNMENT CLAIMS ONLY)* YES NO	27 TOTAL CHARGE	28 AMOUNT PAID	29 BALANCE DUE
	30 YOUR SOCIAL SECURITY NO	31 PHYSICIAN'S OR SUPPLIER'S NAME, ADDRESS, ZIP CODE & TELEPHONE NO		
SIGNED DATE				
32 YOUR PATIENT'S ACCOUNT NO	33 YOUR EMPLOYER I.D. NO			
		I.D. NO		

● PLACE OF SERVICE CODES

1 — (IH) — INPATIENT HOSPITAL	7 — (NH) — NURSING HOME
2 — (OH) — OUTPATIENT HOSPITAL	8 — (SNF) — SKILLED NURSING FACILITY
3 — (O) — DOCTOR'S OFFICE	9 — AMBULANCE
4 — (H) — PATIENT'S HOME	O — (OL) — OTHER LOCATIONS
5 — DAY CARE FACILITY (PSY)	A — (IL) — INDEPENDENT LABORATORY
6 — NIGHT CARE FACILITY (PSY)	B — OTHER MEDICAL/SURGICAL FACILITY

Activity B: Answer these questions about the form shown on page 228. Write the answers on your own paper.

1. Suppose your mother lived with you and was your dependent. If she is the person receiving medical treatment, where would you write her name, address, date of birth, sex, and her relationship to you?
2. If your mother is the patient, do you put your name anywhere on this form? If so, where?
3. What other information would you have to include about yourself, if your mother is the patient?
4. If you were the patient, you would write your name twice. Where?
5. Who must sign this form?
6. Who fills out most of the information on this form?
7. Why do you think that the doctor has to supply so much information?

Lesson 3: Workers' Compensation

If Jane had an accident on the job or if her medical problem was job-related, she could have applied for a kind of insurance called *workers' compensation.* It repays an employer for benefits that must be paid to a worker for an injury that occurred when he or she was working. Employers are required by law to have this insurance. Workers' compensation helps people who have job-related accidents or illnesses pay their medical bills. In some states employees who have to miss work because of job-related injuries receive a part of their pay. They can have money coming in while they are unable to work.

A worker injured on the job applies for workers' compensation. A board studies his application and medical records and decides whether or not he is entitled to get these benefits. If the board agrees that he is entitled to compensation, they approve the payment of these benefits.

Shown below is a form for workers' compensation. It was completed by a friend of Jane's who works at the same company. One day Fred was injured on the job. Study this application to see how he was hurt.

State Workers' Compensation Board

(Type or print.)

	Murray	Fred	Lee		718 - 32 - 0735
Name	(Last)	(First)	(Middle)		Soc. Sec. No.

786 Strand		Salem	Washington	98310
Address		City	State	ZIP

M	27	Mechanic
Sex	Age	Occupation

Ted E. Baer, Inc.   1550 Desalle   Salem, Washington 98381
Employer's Name and Address

$225.00	11 / 17 / 98
Wages per Week	Date of Injury

How did the accident occur?
While I was changing a tire on a company truck, the jack slipped. My hand was hit by the bumper as the car fell.

What kind of injury did you receive?   I broke four fingers.

Have you been treated by a doctor for this injury?   Yes

Dr. M. Santos   1417 Long Street   Salem, Washington 98323
Name and Address of Doctor

Signature   *Fred L. Murray*   Date   11 / 20 / 98

Notice that this application has several lines for you to describe how the accident occurred.

Activity A: Study the workers' compensation application on the previous page. On a separate sheet of paper, answer the following questions.

1. What is the full name of the person applying for workers' compensation?

2. How old is Fred?

3. Where does Fred live?

4. How much does Fred earn each week?

5. When did the accident happen?

6. How was Fred injured? (Use your own words.)

7. What kind of injury did Fred have?

8. Did Fred have a doctor look at his injury?

9. What is this doctor's name?

10. Where is this doctor's office?

11. Did Fred make any mistakes in filling out this form?

12. Why do you think the Workers' Compensation Board has to know how much Fred earns?

13. Why do you think the board has to know how the accident happened and who Fred's doctor is?

14. If Fred can't work for one or two months, how much pay will he lose?

15. For what company does Fred work?

Lesson 4: Accident Reports

Nearly all businesses insist that when an employee has an accident on the job, an *accident report* must be filled out. Many of these accident reports are similar to the application for workers' compensation. A few terms on their company's accident report forms were not clear to Jane and Fred. Let's look at the meanings of these terms.

1. *Shift* — A scheduled period of work or duty; the hours an employee was working when the accident occurred; for example, 3:00 to 11:00, 11:00 to 7:00, or 7:00 to 3:00, etc.

2. *Supervisor* — The name of an immediate supervisor or boss; the person who is in charge of the worker who had the accident.

3. *Safety equipment* — Protective gear required on some jobs, like welding, require that workers wear safety equipment while they work; for example, goggles to protect the eyes, heavy work gloves, or a hard hat.

4. *Witnesses* — The names of people who saw the accident and can tell what happened.

Activity A: Number your paper from 1 to 4. Match each term with its meaning. Write the correct letter for each number.

Term	Meaning
1. Safety Equipment Used	a. The hours that you were working when the accident happened
2. Supervisor's Name	b. People who saw the accident
3. Witnesses	c. Your boss
4. Shift	d. Protective shoes and clothing

Activity B: Shown below is an accident report form.   It includes several mistakes. On a separate sheet of paper, list the numbers of five items containing mistakes. Describe each mistake briefly.

Accident Report Form

1 Date this report	2 Date Incident Occurred				
9 / 13 / 92	Month	Day	Year	Time	Shift
	9	13	92	9:10 a.m.	8:30 a.m.-4:30 p.m.

3 Social Security No.
356 - 00 - 7611

4 Employee's   Last   First   Middle Init.
Name   Race,   Franklin   R.

5 Job Title
Plumber

6 Home Address
1971 Fine Avenue

7 Phone/Home   Work
555-1111   555-0723

8 Date of Birth
2 / 12 / 60

9 Age
32

10 Sex
Male   √
Female   ____

11 Date of Employment   Date assigned to present job
6 / 90

12 Gross Rate of Pay (Hour, Day, Week)
$ 9.50   per   hour

13 Specify exact address where incident occurred. Also specify exact location at this address.

1000 Blair Road

14 Describe fully how incident occurred. (Use additional signed sheets if necessary.)

The thing blew up.

15 Was safety equipment provided?   Was it in use at time?
Yes   √   No ____   Yes   √   No ____

16 According to employee, what part(s) of his/her body were injured?

17 Employee's Signature   *Franklin Race*   Check here if unable to sign.

Summary

Emergencies in your job may require you to fill out health benefit forms. You may have to fill out a form to have your doctor or hospital bills paid or to get money refunded to you that you spent for medical expenses. Mistakes on these forms can cost you money and time.

If you are hurt on the job, you may have to apply for workers' compensation. If the application is not filled out correctly, your request may be denied. You may deserve insurance benefits, but if you do not furnish enough information, the board will not give you these benefits. It may take months for you or your doctor to be paid if the form you complete contains incorrect information.

While no one plans to be sick or to have an accident, wise people make plans, just in case. If they should become ill or have an accident, they are prepared. Using proper procedures and filling out the necessary forms correctly will make things easier for everyone concerned.

Jane found out how helpful insurance benefits were. Because she had applied for and paid for medical insurance, it was there when she needed it. Because she was careful to fill out the necessary forms correctly, both her doctor and the hospital were paid on time.

The law says that you are responsible to pay your bills. If your insurance company doesn't pay medical bills, they are your problem. You still owe the money. Therefore, if Jane had made mistakes on her insurance forms, she might have had to pay the bills out of her own pocket. Hospital and doctor bills could have cost her a great amount of money. Paying for insurance and taking time to complete the forms correctly are worth the benefits that insurance can provide.

CHAPTER REVIEW

Review Activity A: On your own paper, number from 1 to 9. Then read the following statements. Write *True* or *False* for each statement below.

1. If you don't fill a medical form out correctly, you can always fill out another one later.

2. A Workers' Compensation Board may turn down your request because your form was filled out incorrectly.

3. Incorrectly completing a form for your doctor to be paid may cause months of delay.

4. If your insurance company doesn't pay a medical bill, the law says it isn't your fault.

5. If your insurance company doesn't pay a medical bill, your doctor could sue you in order to get the money you owe him.

6. When you have a medical bill, you are legally responsible to pay it. It may be paid by your medical insurance for you, or you must pay it yourself out of your own pocket.

7. Medical insurance is a good investment because it will probably save you a great amount of money at some time in the future.

8. If you are hurt on the job, you don't have to do anything. You will get workers' compensation automatically.

9. Medical insurance will not only pay your doctor, but it will also pay for most laboratory tests and X rays.

Review Activity B: Mary Jennifer Jones is completing a form to have group medical insurance with the company for which she works. She works for Martin and Son, Inc. She lives at 654 North Grand Street in Shelton, Massachusetts 02067. Her birthday is July 21, and she is thirty years old. She is a widow. She has a seven-year-old son who lives with her.

Shown below is a form for group medical insurance. Number your paper from 1 to 13. Write the information for each item that Mary would complete on this form.

Remember that you can write "N/A" (for not applicable) for any item that does not apply to Mary Jones. Use today's date.

Medical Insurance Application

① _____ ② _____ ③ _____   ④ _____
Name   (Last)   (First)   (Middle)   Employer

⑤ _____
Home Address (include ZIP code)

⑥ _____   ⑦ _____
Date of Birth   Spouse's Date of Birth

⑧ ____ Male   ⑩ ____ Single   ⑪ Does your spouse have
   ____ Female   ____ Married   group health insurance
⑨ ____ No. of   ____ Widowed   with another employer,
       dependents   ____ Divorced   union, etc.?

Signature ⑫ _____   Date ⑬ _____

Review Activity C: Write the answers to these questions. Use your own paper.

1. If an application for health insurance benefits asks for "patient's name," what information do you put in that blank?
2. In what space on that application would you put the name of the person who has the insurance?
3. What information would you put in a blank on that application that says, "Other health insurance coverage?"
4. What information would you put in a blank on that application that says, "Was condition related to the patient's employment?"
5. Why does the insurance company need to know the patient's name and the insuree's name?

Review Activity D: Study the application for workers' compensation shown on page 230. Then, on a separate sheet of paper, answer the following questions.

1. Does the application ask for the Social Security number of the person applying for benefits?
2. Why would the Workers' Compensation Board need to know the name and the address of the company for which this person worked?
3. What information does the application ask the person to supply about the accident? (List five items.)
4. Why do you think this application asks the person to give a full description of how the accident happened?
5. Why is it important for the Workers' Compensation Board to know the name and address of the doctor or hospital who treated the person?

Review Activity E: Number your paper from 1 to 8. Read the following sentences. Decide what words are missing. On your own paper, write the correct word or words that would complete each sentence.

1. A worker who had an accident on the job could apply for a kind of insurance called _____ _____ .
2. This _____ is set up to protect employees who have _____ accidents or medical problems.
3. The Workers' Compensation Board can allow enough money to pay the person's _____ _____ .
4. It can also pay part of the worker's _____ while he or she is unable to work.
5. The Workers' Compensation Board studies the worker's _____ and medical _____ .
6. Then the board decides whether or not this worker is entitled to _____ .
7. If a worker does not fill out this application correctly, the board may _____ his or her request for benefits.
8. This is particularly true if the information that has been left out is important for proving that the injury or illness was related to the worker's _____ .

Review Activity F: Study the accident report form on page 239. Then, on a separate sheet of paper, answer these five questions.

1. What information does the accident report form require about the accident?
2. Why do you think the company wants to know if safety equipment was provided?
3. Why do you think it wants to know if safety equipment was used?

4. Does this form ask for the person's job title?
5. There are five dates required on this form. What are they?

Accident Report Form

1 Date this report	2 Date Incident Occurred				
	Month	Day	Year	Time	Shift

3 Social Security No.	4 Employee's Name Last First Middle Init.

5 Job Title	6 Home Address

7 Phone/Home Work	8 Date of Birth	9 Age	10 Sex Male ____ Female ____

11 Date of Employment Date assigned to present job	12 Gross Rate of Pay (Hour, Day, Week) $ _____ per _____

13 Specify exact address where incident occurred. Also specify exact location at this address.

14 Describe fully how incident occurred. (Use additional signed sheets if necessary.)

15 Was safety equipment provided?   Was it in use at time?
Yes ____   No ____   Yes ____   No ____

16 According to employee, what part(s) of his/her body were injured?

17 Employee's Signature   Check here if unable to sign. [ ]

CHAPTER 14

Writing Reports

Julia Michaels had worked for Linsey-Wolsey Company for six years. She was a good employee and had been promoted several times. She had reached the point that, in order for her to be promoted again, she would have to learn how to do some things that she had never done before.

One day her boss, Mrs. Call, took Julia aside and said, "Julia, I would like to recommend you for the vacancy that will be coming up in the sales department when Mr. Roman retires. However, there are some things that you have to be able to do on that job that you have had no experience doing."

"What kinds of things are you talking about?" Julia asked.

"For this job you will need to know how to give oral and written reports. You will travel a lot, so you'll have to know how to read transportation schedules, compare hotel rates, and fill out expense account forms. You'll also have to read professional sales journals and trade publications," explained Mrs. Call.

"Do you think Mr. Roman would help me?" asked Julia.

"I hadn't thought of that. Why don't you talk to him? Perhaps if you came to work early or stayed late, he would be willing to give you some training."

That very day, during lunch break, Julia went to Mr. Roman. She explained her problem and asked if he would train her. Mr. Roman was delighted to help Julia. They arranged for her to come in half an hour early each day. During that time, Mr. Roman would give her all the help he could so that Mrs. Call could recommend her for his position after he retired.

Julia was so pleased that she went to Mrs. Call to tell her the good news. Mrs. Call was happy, too, but she had something very serious to say to Julia.

"Julia, you have an opportunity to turn your job into a career. If you get this promotion, you will be handling a position that will put you on one of this company's highest career ladders. You can move up in this company. Work very hard with Mr. Roman. This promotion can be very important to you."

Julia was determined to do well and to get this promotion. She came to work half an hour early every day and paid attention to what Mr. Roman taught her. She took careful notes so that she could refer to them.

Lesson 1: Written Reports

Reports are written records that present investigated facts about a business situation and that offer conclusions and recommendations based on those facts. Mr. Roman taught Julia about written reports first. He thought that some people found such reports hard to do. So he decided that he and Julia would begin there.

Mr. Roman explained that people on the sales staff had to make written reports. He said that often the person in charge of the sales staff would just say, "Give me a report on that." So little guidance often left people stumped. To help Julia, Mr. Roman gave some tips for handling such a situation. Here are his suggestions.

First   — Say to yourself, "Why am I writing this report?" "What is its purpose?" Ask yourself, "What kinds of questions should this report answer?" Make a list of those questions and answers.

Second — Make an action plan for completing the report. Set dates for each part of the plan to be completed.

Third   — Collect the information you need to answer those questions.

Fourth — Put this information into some kind of logical order. An outline is a good format to help you organize information.

Fifth   — Sometimes you have to explain and summarize what the information means. You may be asked to draw conclusions from the information and to make recommendations.

Sixth   — After you have completed these steps, write a rough draft of your report. Proofread it carefully. Make any necessary changes and corrections. You have to make sure that the final copy of the report is free of errors. It is important to distribute perfect copies of your report.

Julia and Mr. Roman decided to take these six steps one at a time. The first thing they looked at was how to decide the purpose of a report. Mr. Roman explained that four questions had to be considered.

1. WHY is this report being written?
2. For WHOM is this report being written?
3. HOW will this report be used?
4. HOW MUCH should this report cover?

Mr. Roman gave Julia an example. "Suppose you had mentioned at a sales meeting that customers were complaining to you about one of our products. The boss asked you to write a report about what you and the other salespeople were hearing about this product. Let's answer the four questions that we just discussed."

Julia thought carefully about answering each question.

1. WHY is this report being written?
   "To find out if many customers are complaining about the product and what they are complaining about."
2. For WHOM is this report being written?
   "The boss, who may turn the information over to the products department."
3. HOW will this report be used?
   "To correct something that is wrong with a product."
4. HOW MUCH should this report cover?
   "The number and nature of the customers' complaints being received."

"You did a good job on answering those questions, Julia," said Mr. Roman.

Activity A: Suppose that the chief of sales asked you to write a report on why your company has been steadily losing customers for the last three months. On a separate sheet of paper, answer the four questions that Mr. Roman gave Julia to help her begin to organize her report.

1.   WHY is this report being written?
2.   For WHOM is this report being written?
3.   HOW will this report be used?
4.   HOW MUCH should this report cover?

Lesson 2: An Action Plan

The next step on which Julia and Mr. Roman worked was how to develop an action plan for the report. An *action plan* is a list of the steps necessary to complete a business report. It usually includes a statement of purpose. It also means deciding what kinds of topics should be included in the report and determining how and when to gather information related to those topics. Included in this rough outline is a schedule of dates for completing each step.

Mr. Roman gave Julia this list of topics that might be included in any report:

1.   An explanation of what is being reported
2.   A statement on why the report is needed
3.   A list of what will be covered in the report and what limits have been placed on what will be covered
4.   The definitions of words or terms that may not be known to people who will read the report
5.   A schedule of where and how information will be gathered for the report
6.   Conclusions and recommendations based on gathered information

"At this point, Julia, you will want to make an outline," said Mr. Roman. "You may change it as you work, but an outline will help you to organize what you say. By this time you may have also come to some conclusions about the problem and how it can be solved. You cannot be sure about final recommendations, however, until you have gathered all the necessary information. Then you may include it in the report."

"You will also want to schedule your time so that the report is finished, typed, proofread, and copied on the date that it was due."

Mr. Roman had Julia write a plan for the report on complaints about the product. Here is what Julia's action plan looked like.

An Action Plan for My Report

Purpose — The purpose of this report is to investigate the number of and reasons for the complaints from our customers regarding men's walking shorts (#345-687). This report is necessary in order to decide if the complaints are justified and, if they are, to make corrections in the manufacture of this item.

Data Gathering — I will contact all members of the sales staff with a survey to determine the number and nature of the complaints.

Rough Outline —
    I.   Statement of purpose
    II. Survey form
    III. Results of survey
    IV. Conclusions based on research
    V. Recommendations

Schedule —
Survey to be distributed:	6/12/91
Survey to be collected:	6/18/91
Collection of data complete:	6/20/91
Report written and revised by:	6/25/91
Report submitted in final form:	7/1/91

Let's see if you can write an action plan like Julia did.

Activity A: Suppose that you have been asked to write a report on why your company has been steadily losing customers for the last three months. Write an action plan to help you to write that report. Use the following information to help you.

- The report is due on March 26, 1998. March 26 is a Monday. You were given the job of writing the report on February 2.

- Look back at the previous pages in order to follow the procedure that Mr. Roman suggested to Julia.

Activity B: Number your paper from 1 to 8. Write *True* or *False* for each statement.

1. The only thing you have to think about when you plan a report is its purpose.

2. It is important to know who will read your report so that you can direct your information to those people.

3. An action plan will help you to organize your report.

4. An action plan has three parts.

5. One of the parts of an action plan is an explanation of what is being reported on.

6. You do not have to define terms because everyone reading the report should know what the words mean.

7. An action plan should contain a final outline.

8. It is important that an action plan contain a schedule listing dates when each step of the report is to be completed.

Lesson 3: Collecting Information

Mr. Roman told Julia that getting the necessary information for the report was probably the most important step in report writing. "No matter how good a report looks, no matter how well the purpose is stated, if the information you gather is not complete or accurate, your report isn't worth the paper it's written on," Mr. Roman told Julia.

There are many ways you can get information. You can get data by taking a survey. In a *survey*, you question someone in order to collect information. You can get facts from books, magazines, newspapers, trade journals, and letters. You can also conduct interviews to get information. You might learn information by observation. For example, if a product is taking longer to make than it should, you might observe the workers who are making the product to see what is causing the time delay.

The sources you use for your information depend on the purpose of the report and the easiest way to get all the information you need.

Books and magazines will probably not help you find out why you are getting complaints about your product. However, they might help you to understand why your company is losing customers. They could tell you if your type of business is losing money all over the country. They could help you to decide whether there is a market for a particular product or service. They can tell you what other companies are doing to solve the same kinds of problems that your company has experienced.

Newspapers can give you information similar to magazines and books. Local newspapers can let you know about local businesses and the economic conditions in your immediate area.

Let's see how well you can decide the best places to go in order to find information on different report topics.

Activity A: Listed on pages 248 and 249 are five topics for reports. Following these topics, on page 249, is a list of different sources that you might use in order to get information for those reports. On a separate sheet of paper, write the numbers of the five topics. Next to each number, write the letters of the sources that you would use for that topic.

Topic #1:   You have been asked to write a report about the latest trends in the use of robots in automobile plants. How effective are these robots? How much do they cost? What operations can they do?

Topic #2:   You have been asked to write a report about whether certain changes should be made in a rowboat that your company makes. Will an improved rowboat improve sales? Will it have appeal to a larger group of customers? How will these changes affect the cost of the rowboat?

Topic #3:   You have been asked to write a report about how your company can improve the attendance of the workers.

Topic #4:   You have been asked to write a report about the use of a new fabric to cover the seats of the dining room chairs that your company makes. How sturdy is the new fabric? Will it increase the cost of the chairs? Is it stain resistant? Is it available in different colors and patterns? Would it cover properly?

Topic #5:   You have been asked to write a report about the possibility of building another restaurant in Daytona Beach, Florida. How many restaurants are located in Daytona Beach? What kind of restaurants are they? What is the economy like in Florida? What kinds of restaurants do people in Daytona Beach go to most often?

Sources to Use

a. A fabric trade journal
b. A restaurant trade journal
c. A survey of the sales staff
d. A survey of your customers
e. Books and magazines with articles about the use of robots
f. Personal interviews with customers
g. Letters to the Daytona Beach Chamber of Commerce asking for a list and description of all the restaurants
h. Surveys to heads of companies who are using robots
i. Magazines, pamphlets, and other publications on what companies do to improve attendance
j. Calls to chair makers who have used this fabric
k. Tests your company performs on this fabric
l. Calls and letters to companies that have improved worker attendance
m. The production department of your company
n. Magazine articles from magazines published in Florida
o. Newspaper articles

Hint: You will probably use more than one source for each topic. Some sources may be used more than once.

Lesson 4: Arranging Information in Order

Mr. Roman explained to Julia that, after all the information had been gathered, it was time to decide how to arrange that information in a *logical order.* Any order that makes sense can be used. For example, information in a report can be listed according to time, importance, space, cost, etc. Mr. Roman then explained that there are certain things that could affect the order used in a report.

The first thing you should think about is the people who will read the report. They maybe the kind of people who want to read all of the facts first and read the conclusions last. However, they may be just the opposite. They may be the kind of people who want to see the conclusions first and then look at the information that led to those conclusions later.

The subject of the report itself may be important in helping you decide on the type of order to be used in the report. For example, if you are reporting on how good a certain fabric would be for your company to use, you may want to arrange the information in the report so that the reader can easily compare the advantages of the new fabric to the fabric that is presently being used.

The way in which the report will be used may also help you to decide on the order. In some business reports, charts and graphs are placed at the end of the report. In others, the charts and graphs appear on the same page as the part of the report that refers to them. If these charts and graphs are important to understanding the report, they would be included as part of the report. That arrangement makes it possible for the person reading the report to refer to the graphs and charts as he or she reads.

Activity A: On a separate sheet of paper, number from 1 to 11. Then read the following statements about business reports. Write *True* or *False* for each statement.

1. The order in which you arrange information in a report should depend only on who is going to read the report.

2. You may want to arrange your report so that the reader can learn your conclusions first and read the information to support those conclusions later.

3. The subject of a report can be an important factor in deciding the order of information in the report.

4. Graphs and charts can be placed in back of the report.

5. Include graphs and charts as part of the report when they are well made and attractive.

6. Graphs and charts can be placed in front of the report.

7. Sometimes you may want to arrange a report so that the readers can compare one product or one change with another.

8. Including charts and graphs as part of the report makes it possible for people to look at a chart or graph as they read about the information that it shows.

9. Selecting the right order for information in a report is easy and requires no thought.

10. If charts are included just to summarize information, they can probably be placed at the back of the report.

11. Learning to choose the correct order for information in a report can make the difference between a successful or an unsuccessful report.

Outlining the Report

Mr. Roman told Julia that the best method to use to decide upon the final order of information in a report is the outline format. Mr. Roman gave Julia an outline format to refer to when she makes her own outline.

A Sample Outline

I. Introduction
   A. Purpose
   B. Survey of sales staff
      1. Number of complaints
      2. Nature of complaints

II. Explanation
   A. Interpretation of survey data
   B. Irregularities

III. Conclusions

IV. Recommendations
   A. Discontinue manufacture
   B. Redesign garment

Julia noticed that main parts of the report were shown by the Roman numerals (I, II, III, etc.). Details about the main parts of the report were listed under them and used capital letters (A, B, C, etc.). If details were added under the items with capital letters, regular (Arabic) numbers were used (1, 2, 3, etc.). Julia also noticed that Roman numerals, capital letters, and regular numbers all had periods after them.

The *outline* is like a skeleton of your report. It serves as a means for organizing the topics to be included in a report. Using an outline gives you an opportunity to decide how to arrange main topics and details in the most effective manner. On the rough draft of your outline, you can rearrange ideas until the order of your report is as perfect as you can make it. Let's see how well you can rearrange an outline.

Activity B: Listed below are parts of an outline, but they are out of order. On a separate sheet of paper, rewrite this outline. Put all information in the correct order.

A. Grizzly
III. Fruit
A. Trout
I. Bears
    1. Freshwater
II. Fish
  B. Tuna

B. Polar
  2. Saltwater
A. Lemons
C. Rockfish
C. Oranges
B. Cherries
D. Salmon

Activity C: Rewrite these parts of an outline in the correct order.

1. On-site survey
B. Proposed renewal site
IV. Recommendations
A. Purpose of report
2. Written survey of local merchants and customers
III. Conclusions

I. Introduction
1. Survey of area for proposed new store
B. Sources of information
II. Explanation
2. Projected sales
A. Survey data

Activity D: From the list below, pick the topics that would be the main topics for an outline. Write these main topics on your paper.

1. Statement of purpose
2. Sources of information
3. Recommendations
4. Survey forms

5. Store records
6. Conclusions
7. Interview with clerks
8. Explanation

Lesson 5: Explaining Information Clearly

The next step that Julia worked on was explaining what the information in the report means and then determining what judgment can be made about this information.

Mr. Roman told her that in some reports the writer has to explain what the facts mean. For example, the writer has to tell what the problem is, then present the information that has been found. The writer explains what this new information has to do with the problem. You, as the writer, must make your explanations very clear.

You then have to come to some conclusions about the information you gather. *Conclusions* are final and logical judgments based on evidence of facts. For example, after having gathered facts about how good plastic washers are compared to rubber ones, you may have found that rubber washers are less likely to break. They provide a more drip-free closure and do not, like the plastic ones, create much wear and tear on the fixtures. Your conclusion might be that rubber washers are the better ones to use. Those conclusions or suggested ways of solving the problem must be based on the information you have gathered for your report.

Making Recommendations

In many reports you would next make some *recommendations* or worthwhile suggestions on what your company should do, based on the information gathered and the conclusions reached. For example, suppose that you have found out that many companies offer cash bonuses for good attendance. Such bonuses help improve their absentee record. You reach the conclusion that the bonuses are not really costing these companies anything because they are actually saving money by having their workers present every day. In fact, four of the companies you surveyed said that they were saving money with these bonuses. You might then make the recommendation that your company adopt such a policy.

From the two examples described above, you can see that getting the facts, interpreting those facts correctly, arriving at sound conclusions, and making good recommendations are all very important. If you made a recommendation without having all the facts, or without the correct facts, your company could spend a great amount of money with no result. It would certainly cause your boss to have little faith in your work and might even cause you to be demoted or fired.

Activity A: Listed on pages 255 and 256 are eight recommendations for reports. On your own paper, list the kinds of facts that you would have to have in order for each recommendation to be a good one.

1. Based on the information gathered, it is recommended that we try the use of robots on our production line on an experimental basis at first.

2. As a result of this information, it is recommended that we do not change the design of our rowboat.

3. The first recommendation is that workers be evaluated on their attendance as well as other factors. Employees who are evaluated low in this area should not be eligible for pay increases.

4. Because it resists stains, has a long wearing life, and will increase the cost of each chair by only $5.00, it is recommended that new fabric be used to cover dining chairs.

5. It is recommended that we consider opening a restaurant in Daytona Beach only if we are able to buy or rent a site in the northwest section of the city.

6. It is recommended that we continue to ship our product by train because that is the cheapest and most convenient method for us to use.

7. It is recommended that we get and advertise a toll-free telephone number for our customers to use because this service is likely to increase our business by 32%.

8. It is recommended that we stop producing men's shirts with button-down collars because only 6% of the men in this country wear them.

Writing the Report

Mr. Roman told Julia that after she had finished all the steps they had studied, she was ready to write the rough draft of her report. Then she had to read the rough draft carefully and make all corrections necessary for the report to look as good as possible. The final steps included typing, or having the report typed, and proofreading the typed copy to eliminate any errors.

"Usually you make enough copies of the report for everyone who should get it. It's important to remember to keep a copy for yourself," Mr. Roman reminded Julia.

Activity B: Write your own report. Follow the nine steps listed on pages 256 and 257.

1. Write a report on a job or career in which you are particularly interested.

2. Write a clear statement of purpose for your report on that job. Answer the four questions described on page 243.

3. Prepare an action plan and collect information from appropriate sources.

4. Find out how good employment is in that field, what kind of salaries are paid, the chances for getting ahead in the field, and what kind of training or education you need to get that job.

5. Arrange information in a logical order.

6. Next, prepare an outline for your report. Then write your report.

7. Explain all terms and information clearly.

8. What conclusions do you draw as a result of your report? Include recommendations based on the information that you have gathered for your report.

9. Proofread the first draft of your report. Correct any errors. Make sure that your final copy is neat and accurate.

Lesson 6: Oral Reports

Mr. Roman said, "I began by talking about a written report, but you use the same steps in preparing an *oral,* or spoken, *report.* The only difference is that you may not have to write out the oral report in full. In some cases, your oral report will be given from outlined notes. Other times you will write out a written report. Then you may summarize briefly in an oral report what you have included in your written report.

"The most important thing to remember when giving an oral report is that your own enthusiasm, use of language, voice, self-confidence, and appearance may determine how your report is received."

Be Enthusiastic!

"I have seen many oral reports fail, not because of the information included in them but because of the way in which they were presented," said Mr. Roman. "Have you ever seen anyone speak," he asked, "who looks as though he isn't interested in what he has to say?"

"Oh, yes," said Julia. "Those kinds of speakers are so dull."

"Yes, they are," agreed Mr. Roman. "They don't seem to care about what they are saying. Their lack of interest makes you wonder why you should care. When the speaker is excited, the listeners get excited. Be enthusiastic about what you are saying. Then your listeners will begin to think that what you are saying is important, too."

Use Language Well!

"It is also important that your oral report have no grammatical errors in it and that all words are pronounced correctly," Mr. Roman continued. "When you make mistakes in grammar and pronunciation during a report, people question how capable you are. They begin to think that if you can't use language well, your report probably isn't very good, either."

Speak Loudly and Clearly!

Mr. Roman explained that it is important to speak loudly and clearly when making an oral report. "The report is meaningless if the people listening to you can't understand or hear what you are saying," Mr. Roman said.

Be Self-Confident!

"A speaker who seems nervous and uncomfortable makes the audience feel that what he or she is saying is not true," Mr. Roman said.

"A speaker who seems self-confident, who is sure of himself or herself, has a big edge over the person who appears nervous."

Dress in a Businesslike Way!

"Finally, the way you look is also important. You should wear business clothes—a suit, for example. You should appear to be neat and clean. It is not a good idea to overdress when giving a report. People may become distracted by your clothing or jewelry and not listen to what you are saying. If your dress does not appear businesslike, some listeners will not take what you are saying seriously," concluded Mr. Roman.

Mr. Roman had given Julia good advice about giving an oral report. Let's see how much you remember.

Activity A: Number your paper from 1 to 8. Then write the correct word or words needed to complete each sentence.

1. If your speech shows that you think what you are saying is important, the _____ will think so, too.
2. Avoid making mistakes in _____ and in the way you _____ words.
3. Such mistakes will make listeners wonder if your report is _____.
4. It is important that you speak loudly enough so the _____ who are listening can _____ you.
5. You must also _____ words clearly so that they can be understood.
6. You should give the appearance of having _____ in yourself.
7. You should wear _____ clothes.
8. The listeners may not think very much of your report if you don't look as though you are ready for _____ .

Activity B: On another sheet of paper, list the six steps that you should use in preparing an oral report. Remember that you use the same steps for an oral report as for a written report.

Hint: If you are handing in a written report, your oral report should be a summary of the written report.

Summary

If you do well at a job, you may reach a point when you will need to have even more skills. Rather than take courses, you might sometimes learn from the people with whom you work or from a book like this one.

You may also be asked to write reports. Before you can write a report, you must know:
- why the report is needed;
- for whom the report is needed;
- how the report will be used; and
- how much the report should cover.

You should develop an action plan for writing the report. This plan should include the purpose of the report, the steps for obtaining the needed information, a rough outline, and a schedule.

Once the information has been gathered, a final outline should be made. Then you can begin writing your report. You may be asked to include some conclusions and recommendations in your report.

A written report must be free of errors and easy to read. For an oral report, you must be enthusiastic and use language well. Speak loudly and clearly. Dress in a businesslike way and be self-confident.

CHAPTER REVIEW

Review Activity A: Following six steps will help you to write a good report. Read the following sentences. On a separate sheet of paper, write the missing words needed to complete these six steps.

1. First:
   Ask yourself, "What is the _____ ?" and
   "What kinds of questions should _____ ?"

2. Second:
   Then make_____ .

3. Third:
   Collect _____ .

4. Fourth:
   Put the information _____ ;
   _____ your ideas.

5. Fifth:
   Sometimes you have to explain what _____
   and then you have to make_____
   and_____ .

6. Sixth:
   You have to make sure that the final copy of your report is _____
   _____ .

Review Activity B: The following four questions will help you to know the purpose of a report. Read the problem described in the box below. You have been asked to write a report about this problem. Answer the four questions about the purpose of that report.

1.   Why is this report being written?
2.   For whom is this report being written?
3.   How will this report be used?
4.   How much should this report cover?

Your company produces a children's toy called a Quink. It is selling very well, so well that you are having trouble keeping the stores that sell it supplied. The head of the sales department has asked you to investigate how your company can increase its production in order to supply those stores without having too many Quinks in stock. He wants you to have a written report for the meeting of the sales staff next week.

Review Activity C: Look at the problem described in Review Activity B. Suppose you were going to develop an action plan for writing that report. Answer these questions about what you would do.

1.   What is the purpose of this report?
2.   Where could you get the information you need to write this report? (Use sources like your production department, sales records, etc.)
3.   What kind of schedule should you make? Remember, you have only one week to write this report.
4.   Because you have only one week to write this report, you might need to ask some people for help. Who are the best people to help you gather the information to do this report?

Review Activity D: Listed below are three topics for reports that you might be asked to write. On a separate sheet of paper, list the resources you might use to collect information for these reports.

Topic #1:   You work in the business office of a large hospital. You work as assistant to the business manager. He has asked you to investigate why the cost of laundry for the hospital has increased so much in the past six months. The hospital does not do its own laundry. It sends its laundry out to three different laundry companies with whom the hospital has contracts. The hospital pays for laundry on the basis of weight (so much per every 20 pounds). The hospital weighs the laundry before it goes out.

Topic #2:   You work for a company that sells appliances. Your company has twelve stores. You work in the main office in the sales department. Your boss has noticed that the store on Piedmont Street has been losing money steadily for the last year. He asks you to investigate why. He wants you to make recommendations as to whether or not that store should be closed.

Topic #3:   You work in a well-known department store as manager of the shoe department. In the last six weeks you have gotten complaints about the service in your department. You have enough salespeople to cover the store's schedule and to provide good service, but the schedule doesn't seem to be working well. You hired three new people two months ago. The store president asks you to write a report on why there are so many complaints.

Review Activity E: Number your paper from 1 to 12. The following sentences describe organizing information in reports. Write the word or words that are needed to complete each sentence.

1. The order in which you organize a report can depend upon the _____ who are reading the report.

2. They may want to read all of the _____ first.

3. However, some may want to read all of the _____ first.

4. The _____ of the report itself may be important in deciding the order.

5. You may want to write the report so that the reader can _____ one item with another.

6. The way in which the report will be _____ may also help you determine the best organization for it.

7. In some business reports, the charts and graphs are used as _____ of the report.

8. In other reports, however, _____ are placed at the back of the report.

9. Putting charts and graphs throughout the report makes it possible for the reader to refer to them as _____ .

10. All reports _____ be organized in exactly the same way.

11. The way in which you _____ your report can have a lot to do with how successful it is.

12. Writing a good report takes _____ and careful thought.

Review Activity F: Shown below is information from an outline. On a separate sheet of paper, write this information in correct outline form. Use the information in the section called "Outlining the Report" to help you with this activity. (See pages 252 to 253.) Remember that there will be some main headings, some subheadings, and some minor details.

The Purpose: To decide whether to close Piedmont Street store
It is losing business
It is losing customers
It is losing money
Sources of information
Sales records
Interviews with former customers
Interviews with Piedmont Street employees
Interpretation of data
Conclusions
Recommendations
Remodel store
Hire new manager
Close store
Introduction

Review Activity G: Number your paper from 1 to 10. Then read the following statements listed on pages 265 and 266. Write *True* or *False* for each statement.

1. You should always leave it to the reader of the report to figure out what the facts in the report mean.
2. When you explain the meaning of the facts you have found, you should relate those facts to the problem that the report is trying to solve.

3. The conclusions you reach in the report should be based on your feelings.
4. The conclusions you reach in the report should be based on the facts you have gathered.
5. Recommendations are the steps that you believe your company should take to solve a problem. Recommendations are based on the facts.
6. The conclusions and the recommendations you make in a report should be practical for your company.
7. The recommendations you make in a report should be the cheapest ones.
8. If your report is not based on good information, the recommendations you make will probably work anyway.
9. If your report is not based on good information, the recommendations you make may cause your company to spend money for no good reason.
10. It is not a good idea to get ideas from other companies when you are gathering information for a report.

Review Activity H: Answer the following four questions about writing reports. Write your answers on a separate sheet of paper.

1. What is a rough draft of your report?
2. Once you have written the rough draft of a report, what should you do next?
3. After the final draft of a report is typed, what should you do?
4. How do you decide how many copies of your report to make?

Review Activity I: Answer these questions about oral reports. Write your answers on a separate sheet of paper.

1. What steps do you use to organize and prepare an oral report?

2. If you are presenting a written report with the same information, what should your oral report do?

3. Why is it important to be enthusiastic about the information you are presenting in your oral report?

4. If you do not use language well when making an oral report, what may the listeners think?

5. Why is it important to speak loudly and clearly when giving an oral report?

6. If you seem to lack self-confidence, what might the listeners think about your oral report?

7. Why should you wear businesslike clothing when making an oral report?

8. If you overdress when you give an oral report, what is likely to happen to the listeners?

9. If your way of dressing does not appear businesslike, what may some listeners decide about your oral report?

10. Why is the organization of an oral report as important as the organization of a written report?

11. Most people get nervous and tense when giving an oral report, but they must try not to show such feelings to their audience. List something you might do before and during an oral report to help you appear cool and calm.

CHAPTER 15

Handling Business Travel and Expenses

In the previous chapter, you met Julia Michaels. Julia was being trained for a new job by Mr. Roman, the man whose position she hoped to get when he retired.

The new job was quite a step up for Julia. It demanded many more skills than she had ever been called upon to use before. She was nervous about the new job and all the different things she would have to do. Still, Julia was more excited and happy than nervous. The new job sounded interesting and fun. She would be doing things she'd never had a chance to do before. She would go to business meetings. She would make reports. She would travel.

Mr. Roman told Julia that the next topic they would discuss would be how to handle business travel and expenses. Julia would start by learning to interpret hotel rates and transportation schedules.

Lesson 1: Hotel Rates and Transportation Schedules

If Julia Michaels got the promotion at Linsey-Wolsey Company, she would have to make business trips. It would be necessary for her to stay overnight in other cities and states. She would have to understand hotel rates and transportation schedules. Mr. Roman gave her a list of the hotels in the cities she would visit. He warned Julia that while the company wanted their people to be comfortable while traveling, the employees should be careful not to spend too much money.

After each name was listed the *hotel rate* or charge for a room for one person. That kind of room is called a *single.* The company would allow Julia money for the rate for a single room. Look at part of the list that Mr. Roman gave Julia.

In New York City:	The Newton	$72.50
	The Howard	$97.00
	The Sherwood	$76.50

Mr. Roman explained that the company rule was that you stayed at the hotel with the lowest rate unless it had no rooms available. Then you went to the next higher, and so on.

What hotel should Julia try first if she were traveling to New York for her company? What is the last hotel she should try?

A room designed for occupancy by two people is called a *double.* The rate for two people is always more than the rate for one. Most hotels also have the policy that you must pay extra if you have more than two people in a regular room.

Activity A: Shown below is a list of rates for a hotel. Study it carefully. Then, on a separate sheet of paper, answer the following questions.

The Hotel Crown
1128 Strand Avenue
Chicago, Illinois 60611

Rates

Single room, double bed	$45.50	per day
* Single room, queen-sized bed	$52.00	per day
* Double room, queen-sized bed	$58.00	per day
* Double room, two queen-sized beds	$67.50	per day

* For extra person in room, add $10.00.

---

1. For what hotel is this a rate list?
2. In what city is this hotel?
3. How many possible types of reservations could you make?
4. If you were Julia, which rate would you have to pick if your company is going to pay for the room?
5. If you are going to the Hotel Crown with a friend who will share your room, how much will the least expensive room be for one day?
6. What would be the most expensive room for the situation described in Question #5?
7. If there are three people in a double room with two queen-sized beds, what will be the charge for the room?
8. Will the hotel allow an extra person in a single room with a double bed?
9. If Julia wanted a queen-sized bed, how much more would she have to pay for a single room?

Transportation Schedule Abbreviations

Because Julia would be doing quite a bit of traveling if she got the new job, she would also have to know how to read train and plane schedules. These schedules are often hard to read because they use many abbreviations. Mr. Roman gave Julia a list of those abbreviations to study. Here is a copy of this list.

Transportation Abbreviations	
ar. or arr.	— arrives at
dp. or dep.	— departs at
E.T.A.	— estimated time of arrival
a	— a.m.
p	— p.m.
m	— midnight
n	— noon
ET	— Eastern Time
CT	— Central Time
MT	— Mountain Time
PT	— Pacific Time
M	— Monday
T	— Tuesday
W	— Wednesday
TH	— Thursday
F	— Friday
SA	— Saturday
SU	— Sunday

Notice that in some cases two abbreviations are given. However, a transportation schedule company will use only one of these abbreviations on its schedules. For example, Brown Airlines may use "arr." to stand for "arrival," while White Airlines may use "ar."

Activity B: Shown below is a sample *transportation schedule*.   This chart shows the arrival and departure times at all stops on a given route. Study this chart carefully. Then, on another piece of paper, answer the following questions.

Chicago — New York				
Nonstop Flight #	Dep.		E.T.A.	Notes
176	5:32 a CT		7:49 a ET	M-F
184	6:18 a CT		8:35 a ET	SA only
246	7:23 a CT		9:40 a ET	M-F
273	9:45 a CT		12:02 n ET	Sa, Su
350	1:17 p CT		3:34 p ET	M-F
381	7:43 p CT		10:00 p ET	Su only
397	10:00 p CT		12:07 m ET	M-F

1. From what city do these planes leave?
2. To what city do these planes travel?
3. If you want to get to New York in time for a 9:00 a.m. meeting on Monday, which flight would you take?
4. If you want to get to New York by 7:00 a.m. on Wednesday, April 4, what flight would you take? On what day?
5. You have a meeting in Chicago on Sunday that will be over at noon. It takes you one hour to get to the airport. What flight can you take to get to New York?
6. What time does the 10:00 p.m. flight from Chicago get to New York?
7. Can you take Flight 273 on Thursday?
8. If the Notes column had "T, W, Th" listed next to a flight, on what days could you get that flight?
9. If there is an hour difference in time between Chicago and New York and if it is later in New York, how long are you in the air if you take Flight 397?
10. What is the estimated time of arrival of Flight 350?

Lesson 2: Expense Accounts

Mr. Roman explained to Julia that the Linsey-Wolsey Company did not give expense money ahead of time. Once Julia returned from her trip, she would have to fill out an *expense account* form and submit *receipts* (forms acknowledging the receiving of goods and noting any payment) in order to be repaid for the money she had spent on the trip.

Mr. Roman stressed that she would have to get receipts for her transportation costs. If Julia used her car, she would need receipts for gasoline, tolls, parking, or any other expenses related to using her car on business. If Julia used other means of transportation, she would have to supply receipts for planes, trains, buses, and cabs.

She would also have to supply receipts for her meals, her hotel or motel room, telephone calls made for business, and so on. The company does not reimburse expenses for personal phone calls, entertainment, rent, or clothing.

Activity A: Read the following list. Choose the items for which Julia would need receipts for in order to be repaid by her employer. Write *Yes* or *No* for your answers. Use a separate sheet of paper.

1. breakfast
2. train fare
3. a new belt
4. a suitcase
5. taxi fare
6. 35¢ toll
7. a toothbrush
8. parking
9. dinner
10. a long-distance call to a friend
11. gasoline used in driving for business
12. dinner for a customer
13. dinner for a friend
14. plane ticket
15. hotel room

Activity B: Write the answers to these questions.

1. Why do you think some companies do not give employees money before they take a business trip?
2. Why would a company repay only those items for which an employee has a receipt?
3. Why would a company pay for the cost of taking a customer to dinner but not pay for taking a friend?

Expense Account Forms

Mr. Roman showed Julia the expense account form that the Linsey-Wolsey Company used. He explained to her what information went in each section. Study this form. Review Julia's notes to learn the meaning of such terms as *destination, mileage, lodging,* and *reimbursement.*

<table>
<tr><td colspan="5" align="center">**Linsey-Wolsey Company**
EXPENSE ACCOUNT FORM</td></tr>
<tr><td colspan="5">Name of Employee   *my name*</td></tr>
<tr><td colspan="5">Social Security #   *my Social Security number*</td></tr>
<tr><td colspan="5">Dates Expenses Occurred   *From   to*</td></tr>
<tr><td colspan="5">Destination   *where I went*</td></tr>
<tr><td colspan="5">Purpose   *why I went*</td></tr>
<tr><td>Use of Privately Owned Car</td><td>*If I use my own car, I get 32¢ per mile*</td><td>Taxi
RR</td><td></td><td></td></tr>
<tr><td>Mileage
# of miles traveled</td><td>*$ at 32¢ per mi.*
32¢ x number of miles</td><td>Bus
Plane
fare</td><td>Meals
total cost of meals</td><td>Phone Calls
total cost of business calls</td></tr>
<tr><td>Lodging</td><td>Misc.</td><td colspan="3">Total Reimbursement Request</td></tr>
<tr><td>*total hotel or motel cost*</td><td>*anything else I spend on business*</td><td colspan="3">*total of mileage or fare, meals, business calls, hotels, and miscellaneous*</td></tr>
<tr><td colspan="5" align="center">No reimbursement will be made without receipts.</td></tr>
</table>

Julia grinned and said, "If you are not good at arithmetic, you could cheat yourself or the company. I guess I'd better count on my calculator."

Activity C: Match the terms from an expense account form with a description of what information is written for each of those items. Number from 1 to 14 on your own paper. Write the correct letter for each answer.

Term	**Description**
1. Name of Employee	a. total cost of meals
2. Social Security #	b. where you went
3. Dates Expenses Occurred	c. your name
4. Destination	d. a total of mileage or fare, meals, business telephone calls, lodgings, and miscellaneous
5. Purpose	
6. Use of Privately Owned Car	e. if you used your own car, you are paid at a rate per mile
7. Mileage	f. dates you were on the business trip
8. $ at 32¢ per mile	g. number of miles traveled
9. Taxi, RR, Bus, Plane	h. anything else spent on business that does not belong in any of the other categories
10. Meals	
11. Phone Calls	i. total cost of business calls
12. Lodging	j. total hotel or motel cost
13. Misc.	k. reason for taking the trip
14. Total Reimbursement Request	l. 32¢ x number of miles
	m. your Social Security number
	n. fare for taxi, train, bus, or plane

Activity D: Write the answers to these questions about business travel and expenses. Use your own paper.

1. You use your own car for a business trip, and your company reimburses you (pays you back) at the rate of 35¢ per mile. How much would you get back if you drove 118 miles?

2. Why do you think some employers want to know the dates you were on this business trip?

3. Look at the expense account form that the Linsey-Wolsey Company uses. (See page 274.) What would you put in the column that says, "Taxi, RR, Bus, Plane"?

4. How can you figure out the total amount of money you spend for meals during a trip?

5. How would keeping a log or business diary help you to figure out the business telephone calls you made?

6. What does "lodging" mean? What would you put in that column?

7. List at least three miscellaneous expenses you might include on an expense account form.

8. The expense account form that the Linsey-Wolsey Company uses asks for "destination." What does that term mean?

9. If you are asked for the purpose of your trip, do you think it is enough to say "business"?

10. Julia said that if you are not careful, you could cheat yourself or your company. Why might your employer get angry if you did not figure out your expense account accurately?

Lesson 3: Reading to Get Ahead

Mr. Roman explained that employees who really want to get ahead should read as much as they can about business in general, as well as about their particular area of business. He explained to Julia that the more you know about what is going on in the business world, the more valuable you are to your company.

Mr. Roman gave Julia a *professional journal* about managing businesses. Shown below is part of the magazine article that she read.

Too much socializing by the employees can cause problems for some businesses. Here are some ways in which this problem can be avoided.

1. The leaders of the company should set a good example. If they want to discourage socialization by their employees, then they should not be seen socializing.

2. The leaders of the company should be observant. Generally, business conversations and telephone calls do not take much time. When you see employees talking together or speaking on the phone for long periods of time, you can be pretty sure that they are socializing.

3. Those people who are over-socializing should be confronted directly. Some behavior changes should be negotiated.

4. The leaders should administer this kind of policy fairly.

Mr. Roman had Julia read that portion of the magazine. Then he asked her what she thought of the ideas in the article. They talked about these ideas. Even though this article had nothing to do with the kind of business that the Linsey-Wolsey Company did, it certainly addressed a problem the company had. Furthermore, it gave Julia some ideas about handling employees that she would supervise on her new job. Julia had only a little experience with being in charge of other people, and the ideas in this article could help her.

Julia began to see how knowing something about this problem of socializing on the job might help her in her job. Now she could offer suggestions if her bosses asked her about the problem. She could even quote from an article that she had read.

Activity A: Reread the article that Mr. Roman gave Julia. Then, on a separate sheet of paper, answer these seven questions about that article.

1.   What problem does this article discuss?

2.   According to this article, who is doing the socializing—the bosses or the workers?

3.   What does "socializing" mean?

4.   Why is it important for the leaders of the company to set a good example?

5.   If you observe different employees talking or making calls, what might you find out?

6.   How does this article suggest that a boss handle this problem?

7.   Why is it important for the boss to be fair about solving this problem?

Activity B: Suppose you were a boss. Why would you want your employees to read as many professional journals and magazines as possible? Write a short paragraph that gives several reasons why reading professional journals is important. Use your own paper.

Summary

You may have a job that requires that you travel. As a rule, the company that you work for will pay your expenses for business travel. However, you must keep track of how much you spend and you must follow company rules about business travel and expenses.

If you travel as part of your job, you will have to follow schedules for planes, trains, buses, and taxis. You must also know how to fill out expense account forms so that your company will pay for your business expenses.

Finally, knowing what is going on in the business world will also help you to get ahead in your job. You need to know what new things are happening and what is working well in business. One way to keep informed is to read professional journals. Being informed about the business for which you work will let you make helpful suggestions that show your bosses you are interested in your job and in your company.

CHAPTER REVIEW

Review Activity A: On a separate sheet of paper, number from 1 to 20. Then match the transportation schedule abbreviations in the first column with their definitions in the second column. Write the letter of the correct meaning next to the number of the abbreviation.

Hint: You may use some letters more than once.

Abbreviations	**Definitions**
1. ar.	a. arrives at
2. SU	b. departs at
3. CT	c. estimated time of arrival
4. a	d. a.m.
5. W	e. p.m.
6. E.T.A.	f. midnight
7. PT	g. noon
8. SA	h. Eastern Time
9. T	i. Central Time
10. m	j. Mountain Time
11. dep.	k. Pacific Time
12. TH	l. Monday
13. arr.	m. Tuesday
14. p	n. Wednesday
15. n	o. Thursday
16. M	p. Friday
17. dp.	q. Saturday
18. MT	r. Sunday
19. F	
20. ET	

Review Activity B: Shown below is a list of rates for a hotel. Study this list carefully. Then, on a separate sheet of paper, answer the following questions.

SMITH'S HOTEL
1000 Wright Street
Denver, Colorado 80213
Rates

Single room, single bed	$35.00 per day
Single room, double bed	$37.50 per day
* Double room, double bed	$45.00 per day
* Double room, queen-sized bed	$47.50 per day
* Double room, two queen-sized beds	$52.50 per day

* For extra person in room, add $12.00.

---

1. In what city and state is this hotel located?
2. For one person in a room, what two choices do you have? Which is the less expensive choice?
3. Will the hotel put an extra person in a single room?
4. What will it cost for two days in a double room with one queen-sized bed?
5. What will it cost for one day in a double room with two queen-sized beds and three people?
6. What is the least expensive room two people can rent?
7. Suppose you and a friend stayed at this hotel overnight in a room with one queen-sized bed. How much would each of you pay if you split the cost of the room in half?
8. Suppose you had to stay in Denver for a week. How much would it cost you to stay at Smith's Hotel in a room with a single bed?
9. If there are three of you who want to stay in the same room, what is the least expensive rate you can get?

Review Activity C: Shown below is a sample transportation schedule. Study this schedule carefully. Then, on another piece of paper, answer the following questions.

Louisville to Los Angeles Nonstop			
Flight #	Dp.	Ar.	Notes
32	6:15 a ET	9:35 a PT	M-F only
57	9:33 a ET	12:53 n PT	SA, SU only
144	1:15 p ET	4:35 p PT	M-F only
76	2:10 p ET	5:30 p PT	Th, F, SA only
117	5:22 p ET	8:32 p PT	T, W only

1. From what city do these planes leave?
2. To what city do they travel?
3. Do they make any stops between Louisville and Los Angeles?
4. On what days can you take Flight 57?
5. You need to be in Los Angeles for a business appointment at 1:00 p.m. on Tuesday. What flight would you take out of Louisville?
6. Which flights run every weekday?
7. Which flight runs only on weekends?
8. Mary is flying to Los Angeles for her sister's wedding on Sunday. She can afford to stay only one night. Which flight or flights could she take?
9. Which times are Eastern Time? Which times are Pacific Time?
10. Bill has an important business meeting in Los Angeles at 9:00 a.m. on Tuesday morning. Which flight should he take? When does it leave?
11. You can get a cheaper ticket if you take Flight 76. What days can you take that flight? What time would you leave Louisville? What time would you arrive in Los Angeles?

Review Activity D: Number your paper from 1 to 13. Write *True* or *False* for each statement.

1. If you use your own car for business travel, you need to keep track of how many miles you travel.

2. Many companies will repay you if you have to use a taxi.

3. You can be repaid for all of the telephone calls you make.

4. On an expense account form, you can include a package of candy under miscellaneous expenses.

5. You can include paper you bought to make a chart for the report that you are doing for your company.

6. The term "reimburse" means to repay someone for expenses.

7. Some expense account forms ask for the dates the expense occurred and where you were going on the trip.

8. The purpose of your travel is the specific reason why you went on the trip; for example, to make a report or to get an order from a customer.

9. Company supervisors insist on receipts for nearly all expenses because the bosses are mean.

10. The term "mileage" means the number of miles that you drove on business.

11. If you drive your own car, you may be reimbursed for gasoline and tolls.

12. A hairbrush is an item you should put on your expense account form.

13. If you travel by plane or train, the company will reimburse you.

Review Activity E: Shown below is a list of items that Julia paid for while on a business trip. Number from 1 to 11 on your own paper. Write *Yes* if Julia could list this item on her expense account form. Write *No* if she could not list the item on her expense account form.

1. The cost of a taxi from the airport to her hotel
2. The cost of some magazines and newspapers to read during her plane flight
3. The tip that she gave the hotel waitress who served her dinner
4. Two new pairs of stockings
5. Her bus fare from the hotel to the office of a customer
6. A toy she bought to take home to her four-year-old nephew
7. The cost of some folders and clips which she purchased for her report
8. Her breakfast
9. The cost of having copies of her report made so that she would have a copy for each person at the meeting
10. A double room in the hotel (A single room was not available.)
11. A new blouse so that she would look her best at the meeting

Review Activity F: Answer the following questions about expense accounts. Write your answers on a separate sheet of paper.

1. Why must people who work for Julia's company make sure that they have enough money put aside for a business trip?
2. What must Julia do when she returns from her trip?
3. For what transportation costs will Julia's company repay her?
4. For what other expenses will Julia's company repay her?
5. Why won't Julia's company repay her for purchases like lipstick, toothpaste, or a new dress?

Review Activity G: Write *True* or *False* for each statement.

1. Employees who want to get ahead should read professional journals and magazines.
2. These journals and magazines are important because they impress the boss and make him or her think you know more than you do.
3. One type of journal talks about business in general. From this kind of journal you can get ideas about how to deal with employees, how to organize your business, and so on.
4. Another kind of journal or magazine deals with specific businesses, such as insurance or retail sales.
5. The more you read about the business world, the more valuable you may be to your employer.
6. You should not mention to anyone that you are reading business magazines and journals.

Review Activity H: Listed below are ten titles of articles from professional journals. If you were in the real estate business, which of these articles would you read? Write *Yes* or *No* for each answer.

1. "A Different Approach to Selling Houses"
2. "Getting the People on Your Assembly Line Out of Their Rut"
3. "Selling Land: A New Selling Point"
4. "Getting Along With Customers"
5. "Making a Profit From Selling Thread"
6. "Selling Real Estate and Dealing With the Competition"
7. "Tension: Use It For You, Not Against You"
8. "The Life of a Contractor Is Not Easy"
9. "New Ideas in the World of Retail Sales"
10. "Real Estate: The Best Investment"

Glossary

A

Abbreviations—the shortened forms of written words; for example, *req.* for "required"

Accident report—a form that must be completed when an employee has an accident on the job

Action plan—a list of the steps necessary to complete a business report; it usually includes a statement of purpose, methods for gathering information, rough outline of procedures, and schedule of dates for completing each step

Address—the place where a person lives or works

Adult education—classes or correspondence courses for adults. They may be taken to learn special skills such as typing and tailoring, to complete high school, or to learn more information.

Agenda—a list of topics to be discussed (in given order) at a meeting

Allowances—things the government will consider when deciding what amount of money will be withheld from one's salary as income tax (See **personal allowances** for examples.)

Alphabetical order—arranged in the order of the letters of the alphabet (A, B, C, etc.)

Amount—on a sales slip, the product of the number purchased times the unit price; for example, 5 items x $2.40 for each = an amount of $12.00

Apprenticeship program—a situation in which people learn a trade by working on the job; they gain practical experience under the supervision of skilled workers

Area code—a three-digit number that identifies each telephone service area in a country

B

Bar graph—a diagram that uses lines and shaded areas to present and compare information

Benefits—payments or services provided for the workers by the company; for example, vacation, retirement, life insurance, health insurance, etc.

Body—the part of a letter that tells why it is being written

Business machines—equipment used by many companies; for example, a photocopy machine, a personal computer, or a 10-key calculator

C

Career goals—what you eventually hope to become in your business; after years of training you may want to become a master plumber or to manage a clothing store

Catalog—a listing of items arranged in a systematic way; a description of these items is sometimes included

Central telephone switchboard—equipment used to connect or transfer business telephone calls

Chart—a diagram that presents information in table or list form

Checklist—a list you can go over to see if you have completed all the steps you had to do

Classified ads—advertisements that are listed in the newspaper in different classifications or groups. For example, ads for cars would be listed together in one section, ads for pets in another, or job openings in another.

College—the name of the college or university attended

College application—a form used to request admission to college as a degree candidate

Communication—the way or ways you use to let people know how you feel about something. There can be verbal communication (such as speaking and writing) and nonverbal communication (such as body language).

Company—the place where you work or the places where you have worked before

Complimentary close—the part of a letter that provides a polite ending; for example, *Sincerely,* or *Respectfully yours,*

Computer printout—a printed record produced automatically by a computer

Conclusions—final and logical judgments based on facts

286

Counselor—a person at an employment agency or job placement center who helps another person to find a job; a person who gives advice to someone

Course—the subject in which you majored in school; for example, high school programs might include academic, college preparatory, business, auto mechanics, general course, etc.

Course description—an explanation of what is taught in a course; usually found in the catalog

Course number—a number given to a course to show it is different from other courses

Course title—the name of a course: for example, "Computers for the Beginner" or "Computers I"

Credit—points given by a college to a student who has successfully finished a course

D

Date—the part of a letter that tells when it was written

Deductible—a clause in an insurance policy that makes you responsible for paying a certain amount of a loss. For example, if your car is damaged in an accident, you might have to pay the first $100 to have it fixed. The insurance company would pay the rest.

Deductions—expenses considered when determining taxable income; you do not have to pay income taxes on such expenses as donations to charity, qualifying home mortgage interest payments, state and local taxes, etc.

Degree—an award offered after completing a two-year community or four-year regular college; for example, an A.A. or Associate of Arts degree, B.A. or Bachelor of Arts degree, or B.S. or Bachelor of Science degree

Degree candidate—someone seeking to complete a degree program and earn a college diploma

Degree desired—the degree program that a student is working to complete; for example, A.A., B.A., B.S., etc.

Dependents—children or other people who may not work and who count on you for over half of their needs (food, clothing, shelter, etc.)

Destination—the place to which one is going or has gone

Disconnected—not connected; a term describing a telephone connection that has been severed or ended

Double—a hotel or motel room for two people; the cost for a double is higher than for a single

Draft—the first copy of a piece of writing; that piece will have to be revised, proofread, and corrected before a final copy is made

E

Employee (insuree)—on an insurance form, the name of the worker or person who has the insurance

Employment agency—company that is in business to help people find jobs; most agencies charge a fee to either the employer or the employee for their services

Evaluation—a judgment about how well a worker does a job. Many companies use a standard form to judge all employees on a regular basis. This evaluation can be used to recommend workers for promotions, raises, or firing.

Exemption—some reason why a certain amount of money does not have to be taken from your salary for income tax. It might be because you have a child or support a parent.

Expense account—a form on which employees list business expenses so that the company can pay them back

Experience—a term referring to other jobs that you have held; job experience might include dates, company names and addresses, job titles and duties, supervisors' names, and reasons for leaving

Extension—an extra telephone connected to the principal line; the number to connect to such a telephone line

Extracurricular—a term used to describe activities outside the regular school curriculum; for example, sports teams, school newspaper, school play or musical, debating club, etc.

F

Fact sheet—information about you; it should have

personal, career, and educational information plus references. The fact sheet will help you write your résumé and should be kept up to date.

Follow-up letter—a second letter written to correct a mistake, to give or ask for additional information, or to suggest solutions to a problem

Foreman—a chief and often specially trained workman who leads a gang or crew; a person in authority over a group of workers, an operation, or a section of the plant

Full block style—a form of business writing in which all parts of the letter are written against the left margin; no paragraphs are indented

G

Good impression—thinking well of someone because they use proper behavior, language, etc.

Group insurance—insurance purchased for a large group of people, such as the employees of a company; the cost of group insurance is less expensive than individual insurance

H

Help-wanted ads—advertisements for employment or job openings

Hotel rate—the charge for renting a hotel room

I

Immediate supervisor—the person who has direct charge of you on the job; your boss

Indented—set in from the margin of the page; paragraphs are indented in the modified block style of business letters

Index (more than one, **indexes**)—a list of items that are found in a book and the page numbers where those items may be found. The index is usually found in the back of a book.

Inside address—part of the letter that includes the complete name and address of the person or company to which the message is being written

Insurance coverage—benefits included within the scope of an insurance policy or protective plan; the risks covered by the terms of an insurance contract

Insuree (employee)—on an insurance form, the name of the worker or person who has the insurance

Intercom—a two-way system that has a microphone and loudspeaker that allows people in nearby office areas to talk to each other without leaving their desks

Inventories—lists of the amount of goods or materials on hand; stock

Invoice—a form containing a list of the goods sold. Some invoices also have the price of each item and the conditions of sale

Item number—the figure used to identify each separate item sold by a company; used in inventory lists, in catalogs, on sales slips, etc.

J

Job application—a form used in making a request to be hired

Job interview—a meeting during which the person doing the hiring asks questions and rates the answers of the person wanting the job

Job placement office—city or state office where one can obtain help in finding a job; public job centers do not usually charge for their services

K

Key words—important words that give the main idea; clues or aids used to help one remember information

L

Labels—words or abbreviations attached to objects in order to identify or describe them

Letters of application—letters used in making a request to be hired. People writing this kind of letter may send a copy of their resumé with the letter.

Lockers—cupboards or compartments that may be closed with a lock; compartments where one can store personal belongings

Lodging—the place where one stayed; a hotel or motel

Logical order—arranging information in an order that makes sense; for example, according to time, importance, space, cost, etc.

M

Major headings—the most important items in a list; in an index, these items are usually typed against the left margin and begin with uppercase, or capital, letters

Margin—the outside edge of a page on which there is no writing or printing

Maximum—the most; the largest amount

Medical insurance—protection to help pay bills caused by illness or injury. The person who carries the insurance must pay premiums regularly, and the insurance company will promise to pay certain medical bills.

Message—a written or a spoken form of communication

Mileage—the number of miles traveled on a given trip

Minimum—the least; the smallest amount

Minutes—the official written record of what happens at a meeting

Modified block style—a form of business writing in which the return address, date, complimentary close, and signature are lined up near the center of the page; paragraphs are indented

Motion—a formal call for action or a proposal made at a meeting. For example, someone might say, "I make a motion that we spend $10,000 for advertising."

O

Objective—not influenced by personal feelings, prejudices, etc.; for example, you might make an objective decision based on facts and nothing else. An objective might also be a goal, what you aim for; you might have as your career objective to become president of the company.

Operator—a person who uses equipment, or someone who connects and transfers telephone calls

Oral directions—instructions given by word of mouth; spoken rather than written orders

Oral report—a report given by word of mouth; a spoken account either based on outlined notes or read in full from a written report

Order—the placing of topics or events in a reasonable arrangement; the order could be by time, importance, space, cost, etc.

Order letter—a letter written to order merchandise from a company

Outline—a summary of a written work; a preliminary account of a project that serves as a means for organizing the topics to be included

P

Patient—the name of the person who is being treated medically

Pay week—one pay period of seven days; it may run from Monday to Sunday, Tuesday to Monday, etc.

Personal allowances—things the government will consider when deciding what amount of money will be withheld from your salary as income tax; you can claim from none to several allowances on your W-4 form—depending on whether you are single or married, whether your spouse works, whether you have dependents or more than one job, etc.

Personal information—the part of a resumé that includes one's name, address, telephone number, etc.

Personal qualifications—traits that help one to meet job requirements; for example, I have a good attendance record, I follow directions well, etc.

Personnel—the part of a company that deals with the people who work for that company. Personnel might hire people and keep records about how well people do their jobs.

Place of birth—the city and state where one was born

Position—job or job title; the name of the job that an employee does or the work for which one has been hired; for example, sorting machine operator, clerk-typist, or receptionist

Post office abbreviations—newer two-letter forms of state names used by the United States Post Office; for example, *TN* for "Tennessee"

Premium—the amount of money paid for insurance protection

Preprinted answer sheet—a form on which students mark answers to tests by filling in circles, circling letters, etc.

Probation—a period of time new workers have to prove that they can do the job. Many workers are on probation for the first six months that they are on the job.

Professional Journal—a magazine related to business in general (management policies, interview guidelines, etc.) or to specific trade areas (medicine, retail sales, real estate, etc.)

Promotion—a raise in rank or position; it may include a pay raise

R

Receipts—the written statements or forms acknowledging the receiving of goods or money and noting any payment

Receptionist—a person whose job it is to greet the public, answer questions, direct people to offices, etc. The receptionist is often the first contact people have with a company.

Recommendations—suggestions based on information gathered and on conclusions reached

Reference books—books containing useful facts or information, such as a dictionary, encyclopedia, or atlas

References—people who know you and who can describe your character, how well you do things, or how you get along with others. They can be people for whom you have worked, friends, teachers, or clergymen.

Refund—getting money back; you will receive a tax refund if you have had too much money taken from your pay for taxes

Registration form—a form used to sign up for college courses

Reimbursement—repayment of money paid by a worker for business expenses

Report—a written record that presents investigated facts about a business situation and that offers conclusions and recommendations based on those facts

Resolution—a formal statement of a decision or an expression of opinion voted by an official body or assembled group

Résumé—a short account of one's career and qualifications that is used by a person when applying for a job

Return address—the part of a letter that includes the street address, city, state, and ZIP code of the writer; also the part of an envelope that includes the name, street address, city, state, and ZIP code of the writer; it is written in the upper left-hand corner of the envelope

S

Safety equipment—protective gear required on a job; for example, safety goggles, heavy work gloves, or a hard hat

Salary—a fixed amount of money paid on a regular basis for work done

Sales slip—a form used by retail stores as a record of a purchase or sale

Sales tax—a tax figured on the cost of a sale. It is a percentage of the purchase price of the goods bought and is collected by the company that sells the goods

Salutation—the part of a letter that greets the person to whom you are writing; for example, *Dear Ms. Evans:* or *Dear Sir:*

Schedule—a plan that shows the time and the order of each job. It can also show who does the job.

School records—files containing information about a person's grades, standard test scores, attendance, etc.

Second—a statement that one agrees to or supports a motion under discussion at a meeting

Section—one particular class, out of several, that may be offered of the same course

Shift—a scheduled period of work or duty; for example, 3:00 to 11:00, 11:00 to 7:00, 7:00 to 3:00, etc.

Signature—a handwritten (rather than typed or printed) name; also the part of the letter that identifies the writer; business letters often include a handwritten signature above the typed full name

Single—a hotel or motel room for one person. The rate for a single room is the lowest rate in most hotels.

Slang—the use of coarse or of nonstandard, incorrect, informal language; for example, *yeah* or *ain't*

Social Security number—a nine-digit number used to identify Americans for government purposes relating to taxes, unemployment payments, old-age and survivor benefits, and so on

Spouse—your husband or wife

State abbreviations—the old, regular, shortened forms of state names; for example, *Tenn.* for "Tennessee"

Subtotal—the sum of part of a series of figures; on a sales slip, the subtotal is the sum of the amounts of various items purchased (figured before sales tax is added)

Supervisor—someone who is in charge of others; a boss

Survey—to question people in order to collect information

T

Telephone directory—a book or collection of names, addresses, and telephone numbers

Time card—a card used with a time clock to record each employee's starting and quitting times during each day or on each job

Tone—the pleasant or unpleasant sound of one's voice; the inflection or pitch of words used to express meaning, mood, or feeling

Total—on a sales slip, the sales tax is added to the subtotal to give the total amount of the purchase

Trade manuals—handbooks explaining a particular skilled job, such as plumbing or electrical work; books describing new tools, methods, or products in a particular trade area

Transfer—to switch a business telephone call to another department or person

Transportation schedule—a chart or table that shows the arrival and the departure times of trains, buses, planes, etc. at all stops on a given route

U

Undergraduate degree—a degree offered for completing a two-year (A.A.) or a four-year (B.A. or B.S.) college program

Unit price—the cost for one item, box, dozen, gallon, pound, etc.

V

Volunteer—one who provides a service freely and without being paid

W

W-4 form—a form put out by the Internal Revenue Service to decide the amount of money that will be taken out of someone's pay for income tax; workers must complete this form when they are hired

Withholding—an amount of money the business you work for subtracts from your salary; this amount is paid to the Internal Revenue Service as part or all of your income tax

Witnesses—the names of people who saw an accident and can tell what happened

Work schedule—a plan that shows the exact hours or shifts to be worked by each employee during a given pay period

Workstation—the place where a person works or does a certain part of the job

Workers' compensation—insurance that reimburses an employer for benefits that must be paid to an employee for an injury occurring during the course of his or her employment

Y

Yellow Pages—the section of a telephone book that lists businesses in alphabetical order by kind of business. For example, you would find restaurants all listed under the heading, "Restaurants."

Z

ZIP code—a number used to identify postal delivery areas in the United States

Index